Praise for The Brzycki Group & The Center for the Self in Schools

I will miss Henry deeply. He has touched my heart and saved my life. He is an amazing person to work with and to know. I am truly fortunate to have him in my life and you are fortunate to be having him.

—Graduate of "The Vision Course for Adolescents"

As this year slowly comes to an end, I wanted to take this opportunity to thank you for all that you have done. It was such an honor to have met you and have conversations with you about my self and life. What you have chosen to do with your life is absolutely amazing, and I hope to someday be half the person you are because to be you would be almost impossible, for you are definitely one of a kind.

The way I think of it you are an angel sent down to help both myself and many others to help us realize that we too can make a difference. However the thing I admire about you most is your unique way in which you talk to each and every student. The other day as I was walking by I saw you talking to a young man. I'm not sure what you said to him; however when you were done he had a sparkle in his eyes. It was a sparkle of hope and realization that he was special, and that experience made me realize that you have a very special gift, and I was fortunate enough to receive the gift at such an early age. I have finally found my purpose and potential in life, and I can't wait to make it a reality. I hope that this isn't the last two months in which I get to talk to you, but if it is thank you very much for everything you have done to help myself but more importantly my fellow classmates. Over such a short period of time you've changed so many lives at this high school for the better. As I was lying down last night, I was imagining the difference you could make on so many lives if you return next year, and I really hope you do. However, if you don't, I'll do my best to carry on and pass on all of the wonderful things you've taught me. Thank you so much, and if your journey at this high school ends in June, best of luck in the future!

—High school student participant in "Self Across the Curriculum"

Henry worked with my handicapped son, who was suffering from physical and emotional disorders, learning disabilities, school phobia, incontinence and a number of other issues. Henry was instrumental in my son's overcoming many obstacles in his life in school and at home. Henry's work with my son was with amazing dedication and commitment. We had been to many therapists, and none could come close to the quality of care Henry offered. I know my son would not be where he is today if it were not for Henry. My son is now successful in life, marriage, and career—I know he would not be if not for Henry.

—*Parent of son who participated in "The Champions Program"*

Elaine took the time to meet with me . . . to critically look at the work I did, give me feedback, provide career advice, and help me realize my potential. Each day I came to intern I left motivated, inspired, and optimistic. Every day was a new learning opportunity. Receiving genuine, helpful, personal advice is something that most students cannot get on a regular basis. I am so thankful that I had such a great mentor during this transitional period in my life. . . . I am very lucky I found such a motivating, positive experience. Through this internship I learned so much about my personal motivations and myself.

—*College student intern coached with the "Integrated Self Model"*

Mental Health for All *Toolkit*

Henry G. Brzycki and Elaine J. Brzycki

Printed in the United States of America. No part of this book may be used or reproduced in any manner without written permission except in the case of brief quotations embodied in critical articles and reviews, and in scholarly research. For information, contact Dr. Henry G. Brzycki, 2352 Park Center Boulevard, State College, PA 16801, or Henry@Brzyckigroup.com.

This publication is designed to provide accurate and authoritative information in regard to the subject matter covered. It is sold with the understanding that the authors and publisher are not engaged in rendering legal, accounting, psychological, medical, or other professional service. If expert assistance is required, the service of a competent professional person should be sought.

Cover and interior design by Rachel Paul, www.lotusediting.com

Library of Congress Cataloging-in-Publication Data
Henry G. Brzycki and Elaine J. Brzycki, Mental Health for All Toolkit

Includes bibliographical references and exercises.
ISBNs: 978-0-9887161-8-6 (paper); eBook; PDF upon request.

Mental Health and Well-being. 2. Teaching and learning. 3. Psychological, emotional, and physical well-being.

I. Title.
Imprint Name: BG Publishing, State College, PA
Printed in the United States of America

To each other

Contents

Contents

Introduction

Mental Health for All through Schooling

Mental health and well-being belong in the classroom. The *Mental Health for All Toolkit* provides teachers, parents, and students with a new student mental health model based on the latest research in the psychology of well-being and student-centered learning. This model integrates social-emotional competencies, academic competencies, self-knowledge, life purpose and dreams, and whole-child wellness, and helps parents and teachers develop psychologically healthy and self-aware students as a part of their educational mission.

Drawing upon more than 30 years of professional experiences as K-16 education leaders, teachers, and counselors, we have developed this visionary and comprehensive approach to student mental health and well-being through self-knowledge.

The *Toolkit* provides three research-based, high-impact practices that empower students to create their own pathways to mental health and well-being through schooling:

- Integrated Self Model (iSelf)—a framework to use in the classroom to understand the inner self of students through cognitive and positive psychology attributes
- Self Across the Curriculum (SAC)—a pedagogy to teach self-knowledge as part of subject-matter curricula
- Success Predictor (SP)—an assessment instrument and intervention tool to help students determine life purpose and dreams

This *Mental Health for All Toolkit* is organized around the three high-impact practices so as to make it accessible to those who want to use or apply these to their particular situations—teacher, parent, or student. Within each high-impact practice we offer examples or exercises.

The Mental Health for All Toolkit is designed for teachers, parents, and students. The recommendations and examples for teachers and parents throughout this *Toolkit* are also suitable for school counselors, psychological professionals, and school administrators. We primarily focus on parents and teachers, because mental health for all is a normal part of the day-to-day experience and it belongs in the classroom, in school activities and in the home, and not just in clinical settings.

The students we refer to in the *Toolkit* are able to do "what if" scenarios and think about the future. Typically these students are in the 4th–12th grades. College students and post-college young adults will also find the three high-impact practices relevant to their lives. And parents and grade-school teachers can begin to introduce some of the attributes of the iSelf framework to younger children.

At the end of the *Toolkit*, we describe the work of The Brzycki Group & The Center for the Self in Schools, and professional development opportunities that are available. Additionally, we make available our *Toolkit* for bulk purchases and digital format, so as to be able to include the exercises in curriculum or lesson designs.

In addition, the *Toolkit* high-impact practices have been used in and further enhance these popular school based programs: Social-Emotional Learning (SEL), Trauma Informed instruction and approaches, Positive Behavioral Interventions and Support (PBIS), among others.

The *Mental Health for All Toolkit* provides for a direct intervention into the mindset of school-aged children and adolescents. Said another way, our approaches were developed to impact the mental health and well-being of students and not merely to change behaviors or used to improve academic outcomes. We feel that programs that use psychological, emotional approaches to impact academic outcomes are seen and felt by students as forms of manipulation because they are not sincere in helping or empowering them to develop mental health and wellness first, as a priority.

The Self as the Lens through which Students Learn

When the self becomes the lens through which students learn, students can balance cognitive with non-cognitive factors to become happy and whole people who are equipped to create a positive life and make contributions toward a better society.

It is critical in our view that teachers and parents relay to students the interconnectedness among mental health and well-being to student success. The need is clear for a new integrated student mental health and well-being model that places wellness at the center, and moreover empowers students to put together a mental mind-set or framework to be able to define health and wellness for themselves.

The research is conclusive and compelling that self-knowledge is the number one protective factor for children's mental health and a positive life course trajectory.

The ability to experience emotions—this is the goal of teaching and learning in the 21st century. Therefore, educators require a tool bag of approaches to impact the self of their students. If self-knowledge is such an important factor in empowering people of all ages to a great life, then why don't we teach it to more people in more places, through our schools? The silence from our education, mental health, and political leaders is deafening.

We know that we can do better, and should do more to honor the goodness within all of us.

Emotional and Psychological Well-Being

Mental health is emotional and psychological well-being. School-aged children with psychological well-being have a lower risk of mental health disorders and physical health diagnoses such as anxiety, depression, obesity, cutting, substance abuse, and bullying, among others. As such, well-being is an important protective factor to impart in a child's life in preparation for college and careers, and for a positive life.

Educators, parents, and students need a framework with a set of methods to be able to impact the emotional and psychological well-being of children in their class-rooms, homes, and within themselves—what is known as a school-based approach. What should educators and parents look for to determine if their students and children are emotionally and psychologically healthy?

The question parents, health care practitioners, educators, and health and education policymakers should be asking is: How do we create people who are emotionally, psychologically and physically well?

Mental health is not simply the absence of mental illness. Mental health is a state of well-being consisting of happiness, finding meaning, contributing to others, ability to form deep and meaningful relationships, cultivating unique talents, and the energy and motivation to accomplish.

How do educators and parents know if their students and children are well or not? Emotionally and psychologically healthy children possess these qualities or attributes (based on Ryff 1985; 1998; 2003):

Autonomy—children are self-determining and independent; able to resist social pressures to think and act in certain ways; regulate their behavior from within; and evaluate themselves by personal standards.

Environmental mastery—children have a sense of mastery and competence in managing their environment; control a complex array of external activities; make effective use of surrounding opportunities; and are able to choose or create contexts suitable to personal needs and values.

Personal growth—children gain a feeling of continued development; see themselves as growing and expanding; are open to new experiences; have a sense of realizing their potential; see improvement in themselves and their behavior over time; and are changing in ways that reflect more self-knowledge and effectiveness.

Positive relations with others—children are able to have warm, satisfying, trusting relationships with others; are concerned about the welfare of others; are capable of strong empathy, affection, and intimacy; and understand the give and take of human relationships.

Purpose in life—children have goals and dreams in life and a sense of direction; feel there is meaning to present and past life experiences; hold beliefs that give life purpose; and have aims and objectives for living.

Self-acceptance—children possess a positive attitude toward themselves; acknowledge and accept multiple aspects of themselves, including good and bad qualities; and feel positive about previous life experiences.

The Ability to Grow and Change

School-aged children and adolescents need to learn how to change their beliefs when necessary in order to create a better future, for themselves and toward the greater good for all. The inability to change one's beliefs is a symptom of a psychological condition known as a "fixed mind-set." Within the field of positive psychology, someone with a fixed mind-set has the aim to achieve validation. The person constantly tries to prove himself, and is highly sensitive to being wrong or making a mistake. So, failure brings him doubt, demeans his character, and destroys his confidence. As a result, a person with a fixed mind-set, always feels anxious and is vulnerable to setbacks or criticisms and feels powerless in the world. Resulting behaviors include bullying; aggressiveness toward others, including demeaning those that represent views other than his own; and letting off steam or expressing himself inappropriately just to release the inner stress and anxiety that build.

Resilience

The ability to develop "resiliency" is quickly becoming an important personal attribute to live a good life in modernity. Resilience is the process of adapting well in the face of adversity, trauma, tragedy, threats, or even significant sources of stress—such as family and relationship problems, serious health problems, or workplace and financial stressors. It means "bouncing back" from difficult experiences.

A combination of factors contributes to resilience. Many studies show that the primary factor in resilience is having self-knowledge and the ability to manage strong emotions, among 30 additional self attributions. You will find methods to develop resilient children through schooling and family in this *Toolkit*.

Violence Prevention

What is often missing in people who experience mental health disorders is the ability to take a deeper look at the inner self, to know who they are and want to become. Violent behavior is the result of Borderline (Emotionally Unstable) Personality disorder and identity disorders. We can help teachers and school counselors focus on teaching the iSelf model as a violence prevention model to all students who suffer from varying degrees of mental health disorders, with the intent to produce happy, healthier people. Self-knowledge is the number one protective factor for children's mental health.

Mental Health for All

Making mental health and well-being the top priority of schools represents a significant change in how we view the purpose of education. Just as surely as they need to eat nutritious food, exercise and learn every day, children and adolescents need to nurture and strengthen their mental health. Fortunately, teachers, parents, and counselors now have access to new teaching and learning tools just in time to meet the mental health needs of today's young people.

We believe everyone can experience mental health—no matter the physical obstacles or socio-economic challenges. When schools focus on mental health and well-being as the pathway to learning, those with mental health risks will be helped far earlier. To experience self—the whole self—is the height of socioemotional capacity and the most important protective factor to impart to children.

The Challenges We Must Face Together

Life for most of us in our modern society takes a toll on our emotional, psychological, and physical well-being. We do not have the mental framework, and associated mental capacities, to adequately meet the overwhelming demands of modern life. This inadequacy leaves most people with increasing and growing levels of anxiety, depression, disconnected to their experiences of joy, love, happiness, and inner peace, and lacking a sense of purpose in life with related personal and professional meaning.

How can we impact the troubling ubiquitous human issues that characterize our society, or at least know how to process the daily bombardment? From children being bullied in schools because of ethnic or social status, to increased heroin abuse because of post-traumatic stress syndrome, to increased levels of adolescent depression and suicide due to increased stressors, to increased incidences of sexual assault and cutting in school districts, to record levels of being overweight and obesity, to mass school shootings, just to name a few. We think we can all agree that something is not quite right in our modern society. There is a growing consensus that as a society we are failing our children and that we are frozen as to what to do when discussing school safety: focus upon gun control or mental health policies. Additionally, we spend a lot of money on many prevention and response resources, such as police training, school lockdown procedures, and community crisis responses—but not on what is most important.

Instead of our schools and communities being the victims of violence, they can be *the source* of teaching mental health and well-being. We can institute newly researched best practices now with the commitment of concerned, compassionate, and effective leaders. We can prevent incidences of violence by young people by teaching mental health and well-being *through* our schools. There are new breakthrough methods described in the *Toolkit* that do indeed prevent future acts of violence, opioid addictions, suicides, and numerous other behavioral based illnesses.

The Decline of Mental Health and Well-Being

The statistics from recent studies are alarming and have reached crisis levels.

A 2016 study published in the Journal of Abnormal Psychology found that 83% of participants experienced depression, anxiety, or other mental health disorders. The study was conducted over the full lifetimes of the 988 individuals, with a total of 13 assessments taking place between their birth and when they hit age 38. A recent American Academy of Pediatrics study found a significant increase in major depressive episodes (MDE) over the past 10 years, especially among adolescent girls and young adult women.

The most recent statistics collected by school districts across the United States indicate high levels of depression and suicide ideation. For example, the Pennsylvania Youth Survey (2015) found that at one Pennsylvania high school, "The most common depressed thought was 'at times I think I am no good at all,' reported by 26.7% of students in this district, with 37% of 12th graders. 23.2% of students reported they felt sad or depressed *most* days in the past 12 months. Overall, 12.4% of students had seriously considered attempting suicide, compared to 16.0% of students at the state level." The survey noted that this high school is not as bad as the rest of the state of Pennsylvania, so these statistics should be alarming. Poor self-image and self-esteem are significant risk factors to a positive and successful life.

In August 2015, the CDC and the Substance Abuse and Mental Health Services Administration (SAMHSA) asked the public to create unique photos/images with six words on how to prevent suicide. Submissions were overwhelming and included attributes of (1) self-worth, (2) the ability to feel emotions such as love (social-emotional awareness and competency).

The CDC's Adverse Childhood Experiences Study (ACE Study) uncovered a dramatic link between childhood trauma and the chronic diseases people develop as adults, as well as social and emotional problems. This includes heart disease, lung cancer, diabetes, and many autoimmune diseases, as well as depression, violence, being a victim of violence, and suicide. Most notably, someone with four or more ACEs is 460% more likely to suffer from depression than someone with an ACE score of zero. Three ACEs increase the risk of drug use by 93% (health care costs associated with drug dependency have reached $11 billion). A man with four or more ACEs is 400% more likely to be a perpetrator of domestic violence than a man of zero. Women who have experienced five or more ACEs are three times more likely to be victims of domestic violence.

We know that young people today are feeling many stresses associated with modern life. Research has shown that these stressors produce issues of concern such as school violence, drugs, depression, obesity, alcohol, eating disorders, suicide, bullying, and cutting, among others. Young people need new strategies to deal with these concerns while going through them. We also know that young people today want to lead a meaningful life, to empower the fullest expression of their best and highest selves, and to enhance their abilities to experience more fully love, pride, happiness, self-respect, and joy (Brzycki, 2013; Brzycki & Brzycki, 2016).

Treatment Is Not Prevention

Treatment is not prevention. While we expand the scope of our interventions and treatment options, we must also strengthen proven prevention strategies. As a part of an integrated, inter-agency, broad spectrum approach to addressing this issue, mental health prevention requires school-based models and teaching, learning, counseling best practices that empower young people to take control of their own well-being.

We have found that within most departments of education, the functional responsibilities for school climate assessments, safe and supportive schools, Every Student Succeeds Act accountability measures, mental health needs, expanding holistic measures of student success, and social-emotional learning supports are not coordinated in such a manner to affect the health and well-being of children in local school districts. Even in forward thinking states such as California, where they are offering SEL practices to 18 school districts as a pilot, they are using a common SEL framework for improving academic and behavior outcomes, not health and well-being outcomes, as is needed.

Mental health prevention requires multi-tiered, school-based models of teaching, learning, and counseling best practices that empower students to take control of their own mental health and well-being, and that reach 100% of students. School leaders can equip front-line classroom teachers and counselors with research-based, breakthrough methods, while informing school board members, parents, and their community about acute mental health needs. Mental health prevention is not a widespread screening process for depression or comorbidity diagnosis. When students progress to screenings they are already in the intervention and treatment phases of support.

Now parents can express their voices to their school leaders and teachers to make certain that they provide programs and supports that demonstrate a shift—to the inner life of children—their emotional and psychological well-being. Parents using our *Toolkit* can do this for themselves in their homes as a way to ensure that they are teaching their children how to be healthy, and to reinforce what teachers are practicing in their classrooms.

Schools are ideally suited to offer student development programs that consider the whole child and will actually be measured on how they do. There are multiple goals of programs designed to promote positive youth development: promote bonding; foster resilience; promote social, emotional, cognitive, behavioral, and moral competence; foster self-determination, spirituality, self-efficacy, clear and positive identity, belief in the future and prosocial norms; construct a healthy and positive self-understanding; and provide recognition for positive behavior and prosocial involvement.

Prevention means that we are teaching school-aged children and adolescents how to be healthy, how to be well emotionally, psychologically, and physically—as opposed to leaving it to chance that our society's institutions, such as family, religious, and community will somehow impart important inner self attributions. As we have seen through the dire well-being statistics these attributions are not being learned.

This is why we have developed this *Mental Health for All Toolkit*, so as make certain that we are doing all that we can to teach our next generation what it means to be healthy. We want to teach everyone how to be well.

Toolkit High Impact Practice— Integrated Self Model (iSelf)

The most direct path to making humanity healthier, happier, and more successful is to empower a shift, putting the self of the person at the center of our educational system and, more broadly, all modern life.

The iSelf model is a new paradigm of an integrated self that we developed during our research on recent scholarly works in psychology and education that leads to improved academic and well-being outcomes (Brzycki, 2009; 2010). The model also draws upon our numerous clinical experiences where the model of self, the theoretical applications, and actual transformations support the ideas presented and discussed.

The iSelf model integrates component parts from self-system and positive psychology attributes. It is a paradigm for *teaching* and *learning* about self-knowledge both conceptually and experientially.

As counselors and educators who have applied the ideas presented in this *Toolkit*, with transformational results in terms of the quality of people's lives and their psychological and physical well-being, we believe that the idea of teaching self-knowledge to all through public schooling to improve mental and physical well-being represents a breakthrough in what it means to be human, with all the inherent possibilities for a better life, for all. In short, focusing on the self in schooling is an idea whose time has come. In the context of well-being outcomes, learning about and through the self is the most direct and impactful pathway to ensure positive outcomes for individuals and society.

Dr. Frederick Brown, a leading psychology of well-being professor at The Pennsylvania State University, offers his expertise upon researching our work: the "Integrated Self or iSelf model emerges from the interaction of current scientific information about the direct influence by emotions, both positive and negative, upon cognitive functioning. These emotions, in turn, are based upon personal relevancy and meaningfulness and are the controlling switch by which effective learning takes place or not. A positive emotional approach facilitates a sense of well-being that, in turn, enhances a willingness to learn. The outcome, in turn, promotes a greater sense of well-being and less reason for persons to engage in self-destructive behaviors. These senseless acts include addictions, cutting, vandalism, and the current developing insensitivity to others, shown by increasing acts of juvenile cruelty and brutality face-to-face and through electronic social media." There is a natural inner dynamic among emotions and thought, learning and well-being.

Mind, Body, and Soul

The direct correlation between the mind and body (mental and physical health) has been known since ancient Greeks philosophized and built systems of education that improved this connection. We can now deliver on the long held promise that human beings through sound mind can take control over their own health destinies. Plato, in his theory of the Phaedo, said, "The soul becomes involved with a body because it desires to live in a way in which it only can if it has a body of suitable kind" (Broadie, 2001). In other words, in order to express our souls fully and completely during our lifetimes, we require a healthy body to carry out this expression.

Throughout this *Toolkit*, we will be defining an integrated self as the combination of body, brain, mind, and soul. By mind we mean "human consciousness that originates in the brain," as distinguished from the soul, by which we mean a core "animating and vital principle in human beings," to allow for more immaterial emotional and spiritual self-conceptions (Webster's Dictionary). In addition, we use two important distinctions when discussing the self and the self in schooling: transformed mind-set and untransformed mind-set.

Transformed Mind-set

A transformed mind-set (or simply transformation) is a deep change at a being level within a human being. It is a fundamental, systemic change in the conscious awareness of self, others, and all. It is a change in the DNA of one's consciousness, understanding of numerous self-components, and freedom to be who one really is, not who one "should" be or is expected to be. It impacts mind, body, and soul dimensions. It is usually characterized by having achieved a state of self-actualization, a new understanding that includes examining and changing deeply held, unconscious beliefs and knowing one's purpose in life as a higher calling in life to give back to others. A transformed mind-set has experienced all the iSelf model distinctions. An untransformed mind-set is the opposite: one has no motivation to achieve self-actu-alization, no motivation to examine or change beliefs, and no interest in discovering a higher calling in life, and one does not have an interest in learning about the self or any self-attributions common to all yet unique to each.

The self is not separable from mind, soul, or body, and is conceptualized as a holistic organism where each component reinforces the other. In this way, if we take care of our souls, then we will take care of our minds and bodies. Hence we have the thesis that we should be teaching children and adolescents about self-knowledge as a strat-egy to mental and physical well-being.

The demands of modern life have taken us away from our sense of self, our under-standing of who we are, and our knowledge of what is important to us. Archetypal psychologist Thomas Moore (1992) puts into context the importance of proactively teaching the self to children, adolescents, and young adults: "The great malady of the twentieth century, implicated in all of our troubles and affecting us individually and socially, is loss of soul [self]. When soul [self] is neglected, it doesn't just go away; it appears symptomatically as obsessions, addictions, violence, and loss of meaning" (p. xi).

Throughout this *Toolkit*, we will be discussing a model of self that is holistic and can be implemented through schooling. The iSelf model, when implemented in school-ing, proactively addresses human beings at the being level or the level of our souls.

In her own medical research into the mind-body connection and how to help people live more fully, founder of Harvard University's Mind-Body Clinic, Dr. Joan Bory-senko (1995), asserts what is common to all human beings is a core self that seeks emotional, psychological, and physical healing:

"Despite our differences, we're all alike. Beyond identities and desire, there is a com-mon core of self—an essential humanity whose nature is peace and whose expression is thought and whose action is unconditional love. When we identify with that inner core, respecting and honoring it in others as well as ourselves, we experience heal-ing in every area of life." Therefore, with the spirit of this quote—that we can heal in every area of life through identification with our inner core—we hope that you and the young people in your care can learn to love themselves and each other more deeply through the ideas and discussions in this *Toolkit*.

Knowledge of the self is the single most important competency to impart to children and adolescents to ensure health, well-being, and a positive life-course trajectory. The self, and in particular the iSelf model, is a lens through which to view and understand the condition of human being and the reality we have created. This new model focuses on ways in which education helps people reach improved states of mental health and wellness. The iSelf model is situated at the intersection of psychology and education, and it provides teachers, parents, and students with new views and methods that will improve the quality of lives in terms of mental health and well-being.

When we discuss the self of a person, we speak in terms of attributes (and, interchangeably in this Toolkit, attributions). An attribute is a functioning mechanism of the self that includes an understanding of internal mind and what is represented externally as an expression.

In Figure 1, we group the iSelf attributes in order to provide the teacher, parent, or student with an entry point, but the organization and interplay of the attributes constantly changes. The mind, body, and soul enhance the attributes, and the attributes enhance the mind, body, and soul. It is helpful to keep in mind the workings of a mobile to simulate the constant dynamic at work.

Mind-Body-Soul

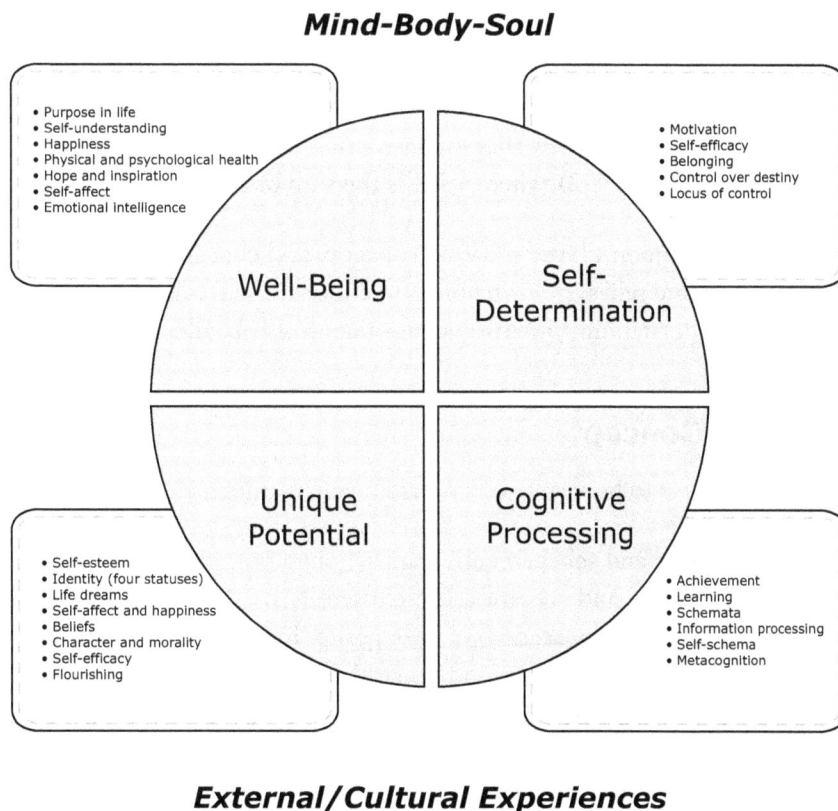

- Purpose in life
- Self-understanding
- Happiness
- Physical and psychological health
- Hope and inspiration
- Self-affect
- Emotional intelligence

- Motivation
- Self-efficacy
- Belonging
- Control over destiny
- Locus of control

Well-Being

Self-Determination

Unique Potential

Cognitive Processing

- Self-esteem
- Identity (four statuses)
- Life dreams
- Self-affect and happiness
- Beliefs
- Character and morality
- Self-efficacy
- Flourishing

- Achievement
- Learning
- Schemata
- Information processing
- Self-schema
- Metacognition

External/Cultural Experiences

Figure 1. The iSelf Model: Component Parts That Include Self-System and Positive Psychology Attributes

The Whole Person

The iSelf model represents what is going on holistically inside a person. It is a way to conceptualize all the components of the self. Each attribute influences the dynamic equilibrium of the whole person.

The whole person goes to school, not just the intellect. Schools and society often objectify children, assessing them primarily based on what is measurable and quantifiable in rigid math and language arts tests. Psychologically, children and adolescents learn that they are not important because their whole person is not being considered— only certain kinds of intellectual skills. They also learn to be externally motivated, through the fear of failing tests or the reward of meeting others' expectations, without understanding the intrinsic rewards of learning for the sake of learning. More importantly, to learn for a purpose—their own.

Self-System Attributes Defined

Developmental psychologist Susan Harter offers an integrated construct of the self she calls the "self-system" (Harter, 1999). By "system" she does not mean to establish a predictable view of how component parts of the self operate. Rather, Harter means to offer a holistic view that is consistent with that of Dewey (1900; 1902; 1916) and James (1900; 1992), where a self is the sum of all dynamic component parts.

Building upon Harter's (1999) concepts and conceptualization, we define the self-system and self-system attributes to consist of self-concept, self-esteem, self-efficacy, self-understanding, identity, locus of control, self-affects, and self-schemas.

Self-Concept

This refers to how you view yourself; your frame made up of important references.

Self-image and self-perception are synonymous terms. Important references can be your interests and activities. These interests are usually grouped or categorized (e.g., academic and nonacademic, peer group, intellectual and nonintellectual, physical and nonphysical, athletic and nonathletic, artistic and nonartistic, among others).

Self-concept most often develops through becoming aware of innate strengths and developing qualities and characteristics and the quality of the experience of performance when exercising these. It develops through a process of attempting to express an innate desire or interest combined with the messages received through the experience. An individual's innate cognitive strengths are commonly organized along the lines of Gardner's (1983) Theory of Multiple Intelligences (MI), which include strengths defined as interpersonal and intrapersonal, naturalistic and spiritual, logical and linguistic, kinesthetic and spatial, and musical and artistic.

Self-Esteem

This refers to the value (high degree or low degree) that you place upon those strengths, characteristics, and activities that make up your self-concept—values such as feeling good or bad about your abilities in math, sports, or music. Numerous scholars and researchers have found a direct correlation between self-esteem and performance.

The following quote underscores the important connection between negative self-esteem and therefore negative self-system constructs and well-being outcomes: "a child who experiences attachment figures as rejecting or emotionally unavailable and non-supportive will construct a working model of the self as unlovable, incompetent, and generally unworthy" (Harter, 1999, p. 13). Thus "the most common affective correlate of negative self-perceptions is depression. In the extreme, depressive reactions associated with negative self-perceptions will lead to suicidal behaviors" (Harter and Marold, 1992, p. 13; Locker and Cropley, 2004).

Self-Efficacy

This refers to your beliefs about your potentialities and about your capacity to grow and learn to become the person you want to become. Efficacy is the belief that you can accomplish a goal. Albert Bandura (1997) and Paul Pintrich and Dale Schunk (2002) conceptualized four sources of self-efficacy that are relevant to our discussion: The first source is mastery experiences, which are our direct experiences of success or failure. Successes raise our efficacy beliefs, and failures lower our efficacy beliefs. The second is physiological and emotional arousal, which impacts efficacy beliefs depending on whether we are anxious or worried (low efficacy) or excited or happy (high efficacy). The third is vicarious experience, which ties our efficacy beliefs to someone who models accomplishments and the degree to which we identify with the model. When the model performs well, our efficacy increases, but when the model performs poorly, our efficacy expectations decrease. The fourth, social persuasion, uses the power of performance feedback to boost efficacy expectations, but efficacy will only be enhanced if the persuader is credible, trustworthy, and an expert.

Self-efficacy is the leading antecedent to student aspirations and career trajectories (Bandura et al., 2001) and performance in the classroom (Pajares, 1996). Indeed, a strong self-system enables individuals to exercise a measure of control over their thoughts, feelings, and actions (Bandura, 1986).

Self-Understanding

This refers to the conscious knowing that you are a separate self from your circumstances, family, society, culture, media, and peers. It is the knowing that you have a separate way of feeling, experiencing events, and interpreting the world, and a personal understanding of your uniqueness vis-à-vis others.

Self-understanding is sometimes used synonymously with self-knowledge; however, this is a distinction with a difference. Self-knowledge is the sum or holistic view of one's self in all of its component parts. In our iSelf model, there are 30 component parts that make up self-knowledge. Self-understanding is one component part or attribute, important in that it allows us to be separate from others and from our circumstances or even past beliefs and assumptions.

This attribute is important in that often we do not have healthy boundaries between ourselves and others, or between ourselves and our control over substances such as unhealthy foods, drugs, and alcohol. Expressions of self-understanding include higher and higher levels of consciousness, awareness that there are higher states and that they contribute to enlightened views.

Middle and high school-aged adolescents and young adults who possess self-understanding grow up to be more accomplished in the domain of school and later in life as healthier adults (Hawkins et al, 2008).

Identity

This refers to your distinct personality. Erik Erikson (1963; 1968; 1980) posited that we form and reform our identities over the course of a lifetime and at different and distinct stages of development. His idea of developing and changing mental schemas inform the iSelf model: an increasing sense of identity is experienced preconsciously as a sense of psychosocial well-being. Its most obvious concomitants are feeling of being at home in one's body, a sense of "knowing where one is going," and an inner assuredness of anticipated recognition from those who count. Such a sense of identity, however, is never gained nor maintained once and for all. Like a "good conscience," it is constantly lost and regained (Erikson, 1980, p. 128).

Building on Erikson's work, James Marcia asserts that there are four identity statuses, depending on whether people have explored options and made commitments (Marcia, 1991; 1994; 2002). The first is identity achievement, which requires the exploration of both realistic and unrealistic options and commits to pursuing a choice or choices made. The second is identity foreclosure, which is a commitment made without exploration (no experimentation with a range of options) but simply commits based on the goals, values, and lifestyle of others. The third is identity diffusion, when individuals do not explore or commit, but rather reach no conclusions about who they are, what they want to do with their lives, or who they want to become as a person—no direction. Adolescents who experience diffusion may be apathetic and withdrawn, with little hope for the future, or they may be openly rebellious (Berger and Thompson, 1995; Kroger, 1996). The fourth is identity moratorium, when the individual is in the midst of struggling with choices, still exploring options, but delaying committing to personal and or professional growth or direction (Woolfolk, 2004). In this fourth status, an individual is apt to suffer from an identity crisis, common among adolescents in middle and high-school, and young adults in college or recently post college.

Locus of Control

This refers to your belief system regarding the causes of experiences and the factors to which you attribute success or failure (Rotter, 1966). There is a critical distinction between internal and external locus of control in assessing beliefs about who has influence over one's life course. A healthy internal locus of control suggests that an individual attributes success to her own efforts and abilities. A person who expects to succeed will be more internally motivated and more likely to want to learn, take full responsibility for the circumstances in her life, and know she can change them to manifest her own destiny in life.

External locus of control suggests that a person attributes success to luck or fate or to circumstances outside of one's self and control. People with external locus of control are more likely to experience anxiety, resignation, depression, and withdrawal from fully experiencing life—to be a victim of their circumstances.

Self-Schema

This refers to a mental model made up of bits of information that are representations of both your internal beliefs and external cultural beliefs known as schemata. The schema organizes the schemata, for example, into beliefs learned from life's experiences. The schema is where meaning is made or processed between one's internal and external worlds to create one's reality.

Our schemas are mental structures that influence our perception of reality, interpretation of experiences, and then how we plan and take action. A self-schema is one's personal paradigm of reality. The self-schema takes incoming information and uses it to create the additional self-attributes, such as self-concept, self-efficacy, identity, meaning, and affect/emotions; it is critical in making us uniquely who we are.

Personal as well as cultural beliefs make up an individual's paradigm of reality and how one sees oneself and one's world. Schema theory provides the critical link between the internal and external self and provides the space for the creation of mind. Cognitive sociologist and Princeton professor Paul DiMaggio (1997) focuses on "schema theory as especially relevant to the representation of social phenomena" (DiMaggio, 1997, p. 283) and "the ways in which social identities enter into the constitution of individual selves" (DiMaggio, 1997, p. 275). Cultural beliefs are integrated into the self as schemata, which are acquired "by individuals during development" (DiMaggio, 1997, p. 280). Reflecting the social construction of the mind, and the inescapable influence of peer groups in schools, family, and the culture at large, Harvard University educational philosopher Israel Scheffler asserted, "development of self-knowledge grows out of the social process" (Scheffler, 1985, p. 25).

Self-Affect

This refers to a personal feeling or emotion that is sometimes difficult to use language to describe because it is an experience. It involves multiple sensations to varying degrees. "Without affect, feelings do not feel because they have no intensity, and without feelings, rational decision-making becomes problematic" (Damasio, 1994, p. 22). Also, "affect plays an important role in determining the relationship between our bodies, our environment, and others, and the subjective experience that we feel/think as affect dissolves into experience" (Shouse, 2005). In short, self-affect is the ability to feel and to know that you are feeling emotions.

Positive Psychology Attributes

The iSelf model also incorporates attributes from positive psychology. Positive psychology is an evolution of the cognitive developmental and humanistic views of the self. We define positive psychology attributes (Csikszentmihalyi, 1993; Seligman and Csikszentmihalyi, 2000; Snyder and Lopez, 2002) to consist of such commonly understood concepts as life purpose, life satisfaction, life meaning, happiness, intrinsic motivation, inspiration, and possible selves, where these contribute to psychological and subjective well-being outcomes (Ryan and Deci, 2001; Lent, Singley, Sheu, and Gainor, 2005) and therefore are important protective factors for teachers, parents, counselors, and health professionals to consider.

Positive psychology introduces more existential perspectives to embrace spirituality, happiness, hope, and dreams. Past American Psychological Association president and professor Martin Seligman (2000; 2005; 2011) asserts that the goal of traditional psychology "was to bring patients from a negative, ailing state to a neutral normal state—from a minus five to a zero" (Seligman in Wallis, 2005). The vision of positive psychology is to bring human beings from zero to plus five and answer the question, "What are the enabling conditions that make human beings flourish" (Seligman, 2000)? This is an important question for parents, teachers, counselors, and all education professionals to consider when empowering the full and unique potentials of all students, from all cultures and backgrounds.

The iSelf model incorporates these positive psychology attributes: life purpose and spirituality; life meaning; intrinsic motivation; happiness; inspiration, hope, and dreams; possible selves; self-determination; emotional intelligence and positive emotions; well-being; and creativity.

Life Purpose and Spirituality

This refers to the reason you are here, for your existence (raison d'être), and describes or includes your basic nature or being: the essence of a human being, the totality of all things that exist, the qualities that constitute existence or essence, and your basic nature. It includes your mission in life as an avenue or pathway to manifest your life's purpose—an inner calling to pursue an activity or perform a service, a vocation, the area of life where you will manifest your purpose. This calling is spiritual in nature and involves a connection with a higher power, an uplifting and transcending force, or feeling of need: to feel the calling to contribute to the human condition in some way, unique to you and your life experiences and views of a better world or greater good. It is what we commit our lives to, bigger than ourselves, using our unique talents, values, and vision in the service of creating a better world. It is part of the underlying motivation and driving force that guides our actions and brings us fulfillment. Our purpose is bigger than we are; it is a lifelong process that we can continuously discover, reflect and improve upon, and compels us to make a difference in our lives, the lives of others, and the condition of the world.

This George Bernard Shaw quote characterizes the spirit of a person's purpose:

> This is the true joy in life, the being used for a purpose recognized by yourself as a mighty one; the being a force of nature instead of a feverish selfish little clod of ailments and grievances complaining that the world will not devote itself to making you happy. I want to be thoroughly used up when I die, for the harder I work the more I live. I rejoice in life for its own sake. Life is no "brief candle" to me. It is a sort of splendid torch which I have got hold of for the moment, and I want to make it burn as brightly as possible before handing it on to future generations. (*Man and Superman*, 1973)

Life Meaning

Today's students are seeking meaningful experiences and a meaningful life. This involves being able to process the vast amounts of information that you take in constantly and then create meaning, a deeper understanding, connecting with the attributes of the self. This is the process of interpreting information as relevant to some aspect of yourself or your life, special to you and the way you interpret life events. Taking information and consciously placing meaning on it can be self-referential or other-referential.

Self-referential involves connecting or encoding with an internal self-attribute, where other-referential involves connecting with external context, such as relationships or renewable energy, usually categorized as "other" or "all."

Intrinsic Motivation

This is your inner drive to achieve to accomplish or reach a desired state. This inner drive may come from instinct, a deep subconscious desire, or a conscious want, and is usually juxtaposed with extrinsic motivation, which refers to the external forces that move you to act. Learning adds to and changes your internal motivations to manifest that which you desire for your best self-interest.

When you learn that you have a new belief about the importance of relationships and you define yourself by this belief, then you are internally motivated to develop meaningful relationships that reinforce your belief system. "Learners who are intrinsically motivated may engage in an activity because it gives them pleasure, helps them develop a skill they think is important, or is the ethically and morally right thing to do" (Ormrod, 2011).

Happiness

This is an emotion of elation, of joy, of feeling that all is well. An experience that is interpreted as a state of being happy, happiness is a conscious thought. The term subjective happiness is often used because there is no absolute state; it is an interpretation of an experience that makes you happy. So while feelings of elation can be temporarily created in our brain with mood-altering drugs, lasting happiness requires more proactive awareness and decision-making. It is often said that happiness is a choice.

The experience reflects a deeper want has been realized. This deeper want may be a conscious or intuitive desire. Satisfaction is an example of a feeling of happiness—evidence that a want or desire or intended result has been realized or manifest. Happiness occurs when the resulting circumstances in your life match your dreams, commitments, and goals for your life, after taking action or implementing a strategy to produce results. People thrive on having goals, and there are always more goals to set for the future; therefore happiness require finding a dynamic equilibrium between your wants and the evidence that these wants will be or have been achieved.

A person's awareness of wants and desires needs to come into balance with her perception of the evidence or circumstances that reflect the achievement of her desires. This awareness and perception are a creative act.

Inspiration, Hope, and Dreams

These all involve a vision of a future state, including all circumstances and emotions: what you can see that you want in your mind's eye. You are inspired to dream, to spark the insight or seed of a desired future state through inspiration either from another person or within your inner consciousness or life experience; you hope that you can manifest that dream. It is what you see in the future, like a dream of what is possible, and a mental image produced by the imagination to see in your mind's eye, unusual competence or perception, and intelligent foresight. "Hopeful thought reflects the belief that one can find pathways to desired goals [and envisioned dreams] and then become motivated to use those pathways" (Snyder, Rand, and Sigmon, 2005, p. 257).

To relate the importance of instilling hope in students and their visions of their own success that includes its effect on wellness, Lopez (2009) provided the following definition:

Hopeful students see the future as better than the present, and believe they have the power to make it so. These students are energetic and full of life. They are able to develop many strategies to reach goals and plan contingencies in the event that they are faced with problems along the way. As such, obstacles are viewed as challenges to overcome and are bypassed by garnering support and/or implementing alternative pathways. Perceiving the likelihood of good outcomes, these students focus on success and, therefore, experience greater positive affect and less distress. Generally, high-hope people experience less anxiety and less stress specific to test-taking situations. (p. 1)

Possible Selves

This is a conception that you can become what you see is possible. It is a thought process where you reflect upon and inquire into "what if" questions and possible scenarios for who you can become and your life direction. You believe either that you are locked into a single way of being or becoming or that you can exercise freedom to change who you are and your life. The possible selves attribute represents your ideas of what you might become, what you would like to become, and what you are afraid of becoming, and thus provide a conceptual link between cognition and motivation. Possible selves include the cognitive components of hopes, fears, goals, and threats; they give the specific self-relevant form, meaning, organization, and direction to these dynamics. It is suggested that possible selves function as incentives for future behavior and provide an evaluative and interpretive context for the current view of self (Markus and Nurious, 1986, p. 1).

Self-Determination

Self-determination is defined by three needs: the need to control the course of your life (autonomy), the need to be effective in dealing with your environment (competence), and the need to have close, affectionate relationships (relatedness). "To be self-determined is to endorse one's actions at the highest level of reflection [and] when self-determined people experience a sense of freedom to do what is interesting, personally important, and revitalizing" (Deci and Ryan, 1985).

Emotional Intelligence and Positive Emotions

This is your ability to discern numerous subtle distinctions of a wide range of emotions, such as sadness and depression, happiness and elation, anger and rage. This involves the ability to manage the emotions with thought and to express them effectively and appropriately within a context. To recognize emotions in others is a quality of empathy or the ability to empathize.

According to Goleman (1995), emotional intelligence consists of the capacity for each or all of these ingredients: confidence, curiosity, intentionality, self-control, relatedness, capacity to communicate, and cooperativeness (p. 194). Positive emotions consist of episodes of pleasure, happiness, energy, confidence, positive mood, enthusiasm, love and caring, and so on.

Well-Being

This refers to your psychological and physical health, where health is not simply the absence of illness, as in mental illness, but the more positive connotation of how well your life is going; your well-being is what is good for you.

Well-being includes emotional health, vitality and satisfaction, life direction and ability to make a difference, physical health and energy to function fully, healthy behaviors such as diet and exercise, quality of relationships, financial stability, experiencing a high quality of life, and living a good life. We refer throughout this *Toolkit* to well-being as the core of a positive life trajectory. So while we include well-being here as a positive psychology attribute, we have been using it to describe the desired result of self-knowledge and the purpose of schooling. The greater good includes the well-being of all people.

Creativity

This involves making connections between ideas or experiences that were previously unconnected (Robinson, 2001, p. 11). Creative people are those who express unusual thoughts, who are interesting and stimulating—people who appear to be unusually bright. They are people who experience the world in novel and original ways, people whose perceptions are fresh, whose judgments are insightful, who may make important discoveries that only they can envision. These individuals often change our culture in some important way (Csikszentmihalyi, 1996, pp. 25–26). Everyone has the capacity for creativity. Being creative involves coming up with something new—for example, a new idea out of nothing that is worthwhile and useful and a unique expression of you.

Motivation to Change

The process of transforming the self of children, adolescents, and adults in a school or counseling setting involves change and change dynamics. An old adage from psychotherapy serves to underscore the first step in transforming a student or patient:

How many psychologists does it take to change a light bulb? The correct answer? "One, but the light bulb has to want to change!"

How then do we as teachers, parents, and counselors, empower the "light bulb" to want to change? We engage the first axiom of structural dynamics (Odum, 1988) that tension seeks resolution (Figure 2). This initiates the change process, the emotional desire to attain a future state, goal, or dream.

Emotions are important because they motivate us to grow and develop and make a difference in the world—the real world. Without emotions and motivated reasoning, change is not possible. When a student knows what she wants, and she is passionate about it for whatever reason, structural tension is created. Structural tension is a clinical term to describe the energy created when an individual concurrently envisions a desired future state, while being completely aware of the limitations of present or current reality. The difference between the desired future state and current reality creates a tension that seeks resolution toward one or the other. The idea of structural tension applies the first axiom of structural dynamics (Odum, 1988) to individual change. In any counseling or teaching relationship, it is critical to establish this structural tension in order to empower positive change. When this tension is created, emotional thought drives the change process. As teachers, parents, and counselors, it is our responsibility to guide positive changes.

The iSelf model, Self Across the Curriculum (SAC), and the Success Predictor (SP) all use the first axiom of structural dynamics (Odum, 1988) that tension seeks resolution (Figure 2). This initiates the change process—the emotional desire to attain a future state, a goal, a dream. This axiom is essential for educators, counselors, parents and students to understand and apply to schooling-based curricula, counseling methods, and mental and physical health programs.

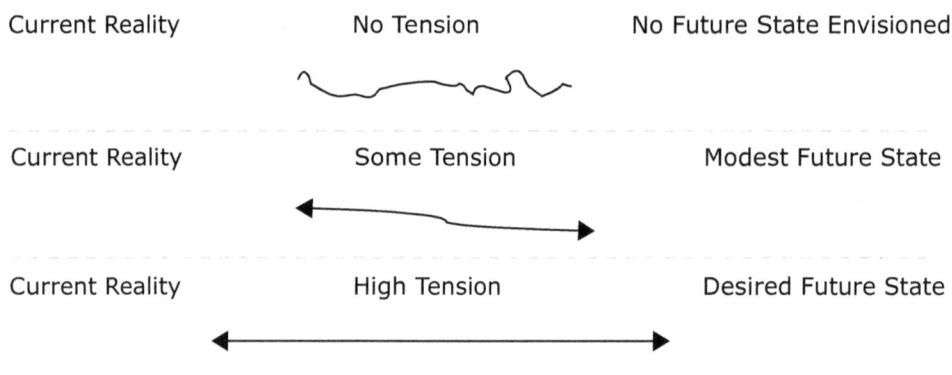

Current Reality	No Tension	No Future State Envisioned
Current Reality	Some Tension	Modest Future State
Current Reality	High Tension	Desired Future State

Figure 2. Structural Tension in Teaching, Parenting, and Students' Personal Development

In Figure 2, three levels of tension between the left-hand side, current reality, and the degree to which a future state is desired are presented. The first level is "No Tension," which indicates that a person is just going through the motions, floating in his life, allowing circumstances to dictate direction and feelings, and self, with very little commitment toward anyone or anything, including himself and his own growth and development. Additionally, he does not have a clear picture of his present reality, either emotional state or physical situation. The second level, "Moderate Tension," indicates a modest commitment to a desired future state, most often with the ability to envision general circumstances such as amount of money needed, new car, or girlfriend. Most likely this person is not able to envision a future state that includes emotions or how he wants to feel as an important part of the quality of his life dream. This person is also not very clear about his present emotional state. The third level, "High Tension," indicates the ability to dream about a complete and whole picture that includes emotional states of being, who one wants to become (e.g., a good person who makes a difference), and numerous and clear distinctions about both emotional and circumstantial future realities. This person also clearly identifies his current emotional state, even if it includes sadness or frustration that the future state is yet to be realized. This person also is clearer about his unique potential in life—something special that he has to give or contribute to others.

Neural Networks

Effective counseling and teaching changes minds and brains in the same way and through the same pathway—the integrated self of the person in our care. In both settings, we are changing behaviors through changing thoughts and feelings that impact the neural networks in our brains. When a student is learning, all these are at work; all are changing simultaneously. As such, as counselors and teachers, we need to be aware of and responsible for our interventions, as they are impacting the self of the students at very deep and fundamental levels. Neurological research confirms what psychologists and educational psychologists already know empirically through observing mind and body connections in action. Brain science is adding to the understanding of these connections by mapping those using brain scans.

In education, mental health, or physical health and parenting discussions, when we concentrate our research or methods only on cognition or cognitive skills, we decontextualize thinking from the emotional self and the consciousness of the whole being. When we feel emotions, it signals an actual physiological state in body and brain, triggering a pattern of behavior that literally shifts blood flow, which is measurable, underscoring that learning is a whole-being process. When children go to school, they come with a predisposition based on their experiences, where all children have both good and bad experiences to draw upon. One of our jobs as educators and counselors is to teach children how to create new experiences through new frames of cognitive thought (which is the basis behind cognitive behavioral therapy and other counseling methods). If we can teach how to literally change children's mind-sets, we can teach them how to enjoy and look forward to the next new experience. They are engaged in life and learning.

Many psychological problems that people are experiencing are due to their resistance to change. Change is always occurring. As seen through the information processing model, our sensory perception is constantly taking in new information and doing something with it—processing it in some way, automatically and unconsciously. More energy goes into resisting this processing of new information than into accepting a new reality and using it for our purposes. Often, we have too much information to process without the proper tools to assist us, so we go numb, unconscious, and dissociate our minds from the circumstances. The term dissociation is a clinical term to describe the separation of our psychological processes from our feelings and experiences. Dissociation often occurs following a trauma, such as childhood abuse, family divorce, and violent events, among others, and in this way it is a natural defense mechanism. Related disorders also help to explain why our youth are in such a critical state in terms of their health and well-being, and include depersonalization and dissociative identity disorder, to name a few (American Psychiatric Association, 2000).

We all know the person who chooses a self-destructive lifestyle: that person who once got or gets perfect grades, starred or stars on the athletic field, and who was or is a perfect child at home, then turns to drugs, alcohol, aggressive behavior, cutting, or suicide. Once this person starts harming, then a DSM-V diagnosis can be made if this person seeks help. But brewing before self-destructive behaviors manifest is usually a lack of a feeling of self-esteem or self-knowledge in one of the dimensions in the iSelf model. Most directly, those who actually do self-harm or harm to others are not aware of their unique life purpose or dreams for their life and do not know how to access either. Therefore they blame others or themselves for their feeling of being stuck in a state of not being able to feel, with severe dissociation.

The iSelf model helps us to first process the abundant information required to live in modern society and then transform ourselves to achieve higher levels of consciousness. Through this heightened consciousness, we can move toward the person we want to become and, more directly, are meant to be. At the bottom line, our job as teachers and parents is to facilitate the change process.

Through classroom lessons, activities, psychological and physical health assessments, or therapeutic conversations, the service provider (whether teacher, psychologist, or parent) works with students, clients, or family members to formulate a desired future state. Importantly, you must keep in mind that change most often takes one of three forms: adaptation between the person and his circumstances, crisis, or envisioning and creating a vision or dream of a desired future state. As human beings, we have the power to choose which way we will change.

The iSelf Model and Borderline Personality Disorders

While studying the association and correlation between mental health and disorders and physical health, coauthor Henry has analyzed which of the mental health diagnoses described in the American Psychiatric Association's Diagnostic and Statistics Manual, 4th edition (DSM-IV), could be readily addressed through the implementation of the iSelf model in either an educative classroom setting or a counseling therapeutic setting.

In one of the cases handled through our counseling practice, "Mary" had been diagnosed with borderline personality disorder (BPD), which is defined and described by the National Institute of Mental Health (NIMH) as follows:

> Borderline personality disorder (BPD) is characterized by pervasive instability in moods, interpersonal relationships, self-image, and behavior. While a person with depression or bipolar disorder typically endures the same mood for weeks, a person with BPD may experience intense bouts of anger, depression, and anxiety that may last for only a few hours to a day. (NIMH, 2011)

Through an eight-session learning and treatment plan using the iSelf model and positive psychology attributes in particular, we focused on her self-image, self-esteem, and emotional understanding of her family dynamics and purpose and dreams for her life. Mary made a dramatic transformation in her life. She went from being withdrawn and angry when with her family to participating in family outings and preparing meals. Additionally, she went on a college visitation tour with her mother, toward whom she had the most anxiety and anger. Mary's BPD symptoms were minimized and addressed at the ontological, being level, and she has not had repeating symptoms in the 10 years since the intervention.

There are many more people of all ages, adolescents, young adults, and adults who are walking around with undiagnosed, untreated borderline personalities. They suffer in silence because BPD is difficult to diagnose and then apply the appropriate intervention. More to the point, it is difficult for mental health care providers to receive reimbursement from health care companies for this diagnosis. This explains why other diagnoses are more prevalent for closely related, yet more acute symptoms, such as bipolar and depression, thereby qualifying for insurance reimbursements. Every day that goes by is another day that children, adolescents, and young adults have not been helped, have not been provided a model of understanding themselves so that they can put into context the complexities of modern life and heal themselves.

Approximately 9.1% of the adult U.S. population has been diagnosed with personality disorders. Personality disorders represent "an enduring pattern of inner experience and behavior that deviates markedly from the expectations of the culture of the individual who exhibits it," according to the DSM-IV. These patterns tend to be consistent across varied situations and are typically perceived to be appropriate by the individual, even though they may markedly affect their day-to-day life in negative ways. What makes these personality disorders so difficult to diagnose, provided with this description, is that all teenagers, when very honest, will indicate that they have either the "inner experience" or "behavior" that "deviates markedly" from their families or "culture," if not for the external behavioral controls established by family, schools, or culture. So, at the inner self, ontological level, to address those inner experiences of difference helps young people feel better about who they are, which leads to improved self-esteem.

These disorders encompass antisocial personality disorder, avoidant personality disorder, borderline personality disorder, and emotionally unstable disorder, and are characterized by the lack of one's identity. Erikson (1968; 1980) and Marcia (1966; 1991) would say that this is a normal process—seeking one's identity—at the adolescent stage of development. We would draw your attention to the use of the phrase "inner experience that deviates markedly from the expectations of the culture" as a very gray area in which to clearly diagnose and prescribe a course of action.

Emotionally Unstable Borderline Personality Disorder

One additional diagnosis where a prevention program would assist is emotionally unstable borderline personality disorder. Most, if not all, people experience some sort of emotional crisis, such as divorce in the family, witnessing or experiencing violence, and emotional, physical, and sexual childhood abuse. Typical symptoms include swinging from one emotional crisis to another, dependency, separation anxiety, unstable self-image, chronic feelings of emptiness, and threats of self-harm, such as self-mutilation, of which cutting is an example. While some children receive the emotional unstable diagnosis, in many cases, we accept these symptoms as normal for our children, in this modern time, in human history. Yet they are not normal—they are acute symptoms of children in crisis and a characteristic outcome of a culture and a society and a school system that is in need of a paradigm shift so as to be able to heal our people.

Approximately 8% to 10% of individuals diagnosed with emotionally unstable disorder end their lives in suicide. In adulthood, job losses, interrupted education, and broken marriages are common. The primary risk factors for emotionally unstable disorder are having a very stressful or chaotic childhood (e.g., physical and sexual abuse, neglect, hostile conflict, and early parental loss or separation). Mood disorders, substance-related disorders, eating disorders (usually bulimia), post-traumatic stress disorder, attention-deficit/hyperactivity disorder, and other personality disorders frequently co-occur with emotional unstable disorder.

We would assert that these risk factors and co-occurrences are common and affect most in our society. The incidences are underreported because we are accepting this state as the new normal: We accept these symptoms, allow them to persist, or treat them with medications without regard to developing prevention programs.

Because we have so many people in the world who will never be diagnosed with personality disorder and teachers themselves are not trained to address these pervasive needs, we need to give teachers and students a better model for prevention. The iSelf model offers a teacher or counselor access to the inner experience and life of their students or clients. With the iSelf model, teachers and counselors and direct service professionals can shift their focus to a student's inner life and experiences when designing their interventions and prevention programs. This creates a healthier balance for how we work with young people—before they qualify for DSM-IV diagnoses.

iSelf Model Implementation

The iSelf model forms the foundation for mental health and well-being; it enhances and strengthens the three high-impact practices by providing students, parents, and professionals with enlightening self-system and positive psychology concepts and attributions such as happiness, purpose in life, and well-being. Further, it provides parents, counselors, and teachers with refined distinctions about the inner life of children or students, the whole person we are working with, helping us read their behaviors, emotions, and reactions.

Teaching and counseling methods over the past few years are merging together. Counseling and teaching provides support to people to help them deal with problems and make important decisions, and guides them using a psychological framework. In the Mental Health for All model, teachers are counselors and counselors are teachers, both using the iSelf model as the psychological framework to empower students.

To be aware of these high-impact practices for working with school-aged children, adolescents, and young adults increases teaching and counseling professionals' effectiveness when transforming students in our care.

Recommendations for Teachers

Teachers can strengthen their students' self-knowledge and well-being in both simple and complex ways. Teachers can make a significant difference by developing programs for students, working with each other across units, and reaching up through the hierarchies of leadership for school-wide change. Teachers can:

- Read the iSelf distinctions and incorporate at least one distinction into an assignment, noting for students when they have strengthened their awareness of the distinction. For example, self-efficacy can be demonstrated by defending a mathematical theorem, and locus of control can be demonstrated by student taking responsibility for the school's recycling program.
- Explore ways to incorporate emotional learning in cognitive assignments, such as connecting assignments to making a meaningful contribution to the community that students are passionate about.
- Form a teacher group to explore ways to encourage and recognize students' self-knowledge and self-responsibility.
- Hold intra- and interdepartmental discussions on the promising and high-impact practices in this *Toolkit* to explore ones to incorporate into classes and school activities.
- Develop preventative programming based on the iSelf model's self-system and positive psychology attributions.
- Create new student handbooks and other resources.
- Build the iSelf attributes into home-room programs.
- Develop programs that support students' developmental progress towards their personal, college and professional goals.
- Design metrics to measure students' well-being.
- Hold teacher professional development sessions on the many ways to impart well-being and self-knowledge using the *Mental Health for All Toolkit*, through PLCs or in-service sessions.

- Make presentations to school leaders and community members on the iSelf distinctions they feel are most important to include in the school's mission and programs.

Example for Teachers

The iSelf model, when applied through schooling, helps effective teachers teach students important self-distinctions using subject content in their classrooms. What then occurs is deeper learning. The self is the context that makes the academic content meaningful and therefore creates a deeper understanding.

Emotions tell each of us what is important to learn, know, and be able to do. It is tragic that our schools have ignored this critical dimension of the self (affect and emotional intelligence) and of learning. It is tragic because teachers are searching for ways to not only engage their students in learning academic content but also make learning more meaningful and purposeful for each student. We need to impart emotional intelligence, self-awareness, and health through schooling so that we can create a more thoughtful and civil society with honest debate about how to solve the real and deep problems we confront.

A recent story from the headlines underscores the need to teach emotional well-being. When asked about the reasons why a group of 15–20 teenagers stood by and watched a 15-year-old girl gang raped and beaten as their classmates filed into the school auditorium for the annual homecoming dance, mind-body healing pioneer and expert Dr. Deepak Chopra declared in a CNN interview that "there is an epidemic of emotional retardation," underscoring the need to teach what healthy emotions are and provide a method of emotional healing for our children through schooling. If viewing the rape through the iSelf lens, at least one of these 15–20 bystanders would have seen the immorality of this event and intervened in a number of possible ways. They would have empathized with the girl and taken some appropriate action. Further, the adolescents' gang raping and beating the girl would have been able to better process their emotions and not taken out their frustrations and anger on the girl. Thus the event would not have occurred in the first place.

Here is a case in point where a teacher and a parent did not know the importance of emotions and the inner life of one of her students. The young daughter of one of coauthor Henry's graduate students wrote this poem in a bell-ringer exercise (a beginning class exercise that focuses students upon entering a class), as assigned by her homeroom teacher (used with permission by the parent):

> Depression overcomes my body,
> suffocating the joys of life.
> Adding on more childish fears.
> My hopes are beginning to flow
> Under the surface of my knowing,
> that usually makes me feel better.
> But not this time.
> I can't function correctly in this life.
> Will someone please tell me what I've messed up on this time?
> Won't someone notice the pain I'm experiencing?
> Please, somebody out there must save me before I drown
> in my own sorrow.
> Please—anyone!!!

The teacher—under pressure to improve standardized tests scores in language arts and having received her teacher training in a traditional teacher education program where the current and dominant policies and best practices are taught—instead of approaching the girl privately to inquire into her state of mind, graded the poem using state language arts standards as her reference. The teacher, though skilled at teaching curriculum standards and teaching to the test, failed to even notice the state of mind of an 11-year-old girl.

Recommendations for Parents

For parents we recommend referencing one or more of the 30 iSelf model distinctions when communicating with your children. Acknowledging your child's grit or resilience is an example of commitment toward something deemed important by your child. Or, when your child is emoting about something that seems unimportant to you, acknowledge their abilities to feel—the iSelf attribution "affect"—and ask what this means. Develop a family mission statement that puts mental health and well-being at the core of family relationships and activities. Determine family rules to ensure that technology use supports the family mission rather than detracts from it. Communicate your family mission to your children's teachers so they can better support your children during the school day.

Examples for Parents

Example 1: Summer Bridge Program Using the iSelf Model

Coauthor Henry, through The Brzycki Group, conducts summer bridge programs for students planning to go to college, whether undecided or firm in their college choices. The program combines personal counseling (self-understanding and esteem) with academic advising (which college academic program to enter), with career counseling (which profession), and student engagement (how to make learning real world). One participant, "Ryan," was diagnosed with numerous learning disabilities that severely impacted his high school academic career, and he barely graduated. By summer, he had not yet even applied to colleges.

Further, he suffered from a severe poor self-image because during his freshman year in high school, given his academic difficulties, his mother decided that Ryan must be hard of hearing, which his doctors determined was not true. She found a hearing device that was worn around his neck and hung down to his chest, with an earpiece going into both ears. This seems archaic, and was. Ryan had to wear this around all through high school and was the brunt of jokes and bullying, degrading his sense of self-worth.

Ryan's parents were high power, successful professionally, and believed—were determined—that their son was going to be successful as well. They had placed so much pressure on him to achieve academically that he literally cried every evening when attempting to do his homework.

Through appreciative inquiry about his strengths, his talents, and his dreams for his life, we (parents, child, and our coaching) discovered that he was very gifted in anything to do with the sea, sailing, navigating using charts and radar, fishing, lobstering, fixing boat motors and carpentry, among others. His self-esteem soared upon learning that he was actually gifted and that these could help him realize a dream, to develop fish farms off the coast of Maine. Further, he gained the understanding that he could determine his future, his own pathway to manifesting his dream. (He deepened his experience of two iSelf distinctions: self-determination and locus of control.) He applied and was accepted to the Maine Maritime Academy, which has rolling admissions and an active learning support program.

Through internships, service learning opportunities at his college, along with additional summer jobs and projects, he strengthened his newfound self-esteem through achievement, and he saw the results that he produced in the world. He built boats, fixed boat motors, offered guided tours, and did hands-on internships where he could gain self-efficacy, the belief that he could attain his goals.

Ryan also learned that being a sensitive soul, having a caring heart, and wanting to help humanity by feeding them and making them safer were all good qualities beyond his academic course work. He was a whole person! He had hopes and dreams that had laid dormant, unconscious to even him, and he became a new person.

He became cognitively (iSelf attribution of metacognition) aware that he indeed had these learning disabilities, and took action (iSelf attribution of self-determination) to obtain the appropriate study skills and organization assistance that he needed. He no longer felt as though he needed to hide his imperfections. Further, he was no longer emotionally upset about not being able to handle the increased academic requirements—evidence of increased emotional intelligence and management. He could also feel genuine happiness for who he is (iSelf attributions of emotional intelligence, self-affect, and happiness).

Ryan went on to major in marine sciences and start his own boating and fishing business in Maine, satisfying his own vision of success in his life.

Example 2: Well-Being Workshops Using the iSelf Model

The Center for the Self in Schools designed a workshop using the iSelf model as the framework for well-being, where a number of key distinctions were discussed.

Purpose in life: Why do you think you are here at this time in human history? What is your unique purpose in life? What have you experienced in your life thus far that compels you to take action to impact a quality or issue?

One student indicated that she had been sexually abused as a child. She went home and communicated with her mother how she had come to understand that this experience in her life, trauma really, informed her unique purpose. The mother and daughter worked on their purposes in life together and then took actions to manifest these. The mother communicated for the first time that she too was abused as a child. As both were sexually abused as children by family members, and so, armed with new self-understanding and purpose in life, they went on to develop a sexual-abuse prevention program that was eventually proposed for statewide adoption.

The mother, who was diagnosed with bipolar affective disorder, with the approval of her medical doctor, reduced her medications after reshaping her entire paradigm of self and her reality and becoming whole again with herself, which created a healthy balance in her brain chemistry.

The girl, with the genetic factor associated with bipolar affective disorder, could have easily fallen into this family diagnosis, instead of gaining a new level of emotional intelligence through her learning. Her learning took the form of writing in journals and poems, diagnosing these from a self-lens, and subsequent short meetings to discuss purpose in life and motivations to take action, demonstrating the effectiveness of using iSelf distinctions when learning about how personal knowledge impacts well-being, resulting in enhanced personal well-being.

Through our work together, we would have seen changes in the brain gray matter of both the mother and the daughter, both in the prefrontal cortex (where, psychologically, executive functioning resides) and in the left amygdala (the brain's emotional center). Therefore, the daughter prevented affective disorders through learning about herself and becoming more emotionally connected, passionate really, about her purpose in life. Many disorders that are often treated with psychotropic medications can be treated through changes in the brain chemistry and functioning, and learning about one's higher purpose in life can literally change brain functioning by forming healthy new connections between executive functioning and emotional responses.

We have found that emotional well-being can be achieved if any individual—child, adolescent or adult—is taught that he has a unique self with specific attributions such as unique purpose. This alone shifts his way of being to more of an ontological inquiry, with a newfound inner peace, and leads to subsequent changes in behavior and experiences of emotional well-being characterized as less anxiety and stress.

Recommendations for Students

Today's youth find themselves focused on external goals such as wealth, fame, success; emotional dependency upon technology; attainment of school-based measures; and college selection, to name a few. Without being able to focus on internal goals, such as feelings, self-understanding, relationship intimacy, and purpose and dreams in life, among others, it is no wonder that young people are experiencing that it all feels beyond their control to live a high quality of life, a flourishing life to the level of their unique potentials and what they can envision.

The increase in mental health issues such as anxiety and depression underscores the need for a cultural and paradigmatic shift from external motivations and measures of success to internal motivations and measures, such as self-knowledge, among others called for in the iSelf model.

Individual students and student groups, particularly those in the upper grades in high school, do not need to wait for their school or families to make systemic changes in order to put well-being and self-knowledge at the center of their own learning experiences. Students can:

- Read and learn more about the iSelf distinctions, and provide themselves with a new awareness of the self-system and positive psychology attributions that have been shown to lead to positive life trajectories.
- Complete the Success Predictor described in the last section of the *Toolkit* to proactively develop a structure in their schools and families to accomplish their goals and pursue their dreams.
- Develop peer-to-peer counseling groups to discuss the iSelf distinctions and encourage self-authorship.
- Reach out to teachers to engage in extracurricular and community-based projects.
- Create groups to meet with school leaders to discuss needs and request resources to support their well-being.
- Continue to voice that the purpose of education is well-being for self, family, friends, institutions, and society.

Toolkit High Impact Practice— Self Across the Curriculum (SAC)

The Self Across the Curriculum (SAC) is a pedagogy that has been used in K-12 classrooms, school counseling programs, college undergraduate and graduate courses to improve student mental health and learning outcomes.

We developed SAC to impart iSelf model attributions when we discovered that students were more engaged in learning when it is self-referential, where the self of the student is used as a prism or the lens through which to view all subject content; thus the information learned relates more directly to other situations and employs higher cognitive and metacognitive functions.

The SAC teaches students how to first understand themselves, and then how to process and understand the content information that is taught (e.g., psychology, math, and writing). What results is deeper learning and understanding of both the self and the subject content.

The SAC helps teachers . . .

- Know how to see "inside" each student and help design lessons that develop each iSelf model attribution.
- Increase students' abilities to be more engaged in their learning by applying knowledge.
- Connect students with the content for increased learning outcomes.
- Demonstrate how to develop rigorous academic mind-sets among students.
- Increase connections between students and teachers.
- Help teachers improve student academic performance.
- Contribute to the school's mission to promote well-being through teaching self-knowledge.
- Contribute to a paradigmatic shift in societal values and the greater good.

Just as the popular Writing Across the Curriculum (WAC) has two simultaneous goals, to teach writing skills through content and to use writing to teach subject content, the SAC also has two goals: to teach self-knowledge through content and to use self-knowledge to help students connect with the content more thoroughly and deeply. This type of teaching and learning requires a different focus, an internal focus versus an external one; it drives the learner to look inward first, to know one's self and attain a sense of purpose, dreams, moral center, and personal strengths, so as to literally create or construct one's self using the iSelf model as a framework. The advantage of learning about the self is that when it is time to develop a strategy to learn about and apply course content, students demonstrate dramatically increased efficacy and creativity when problem solving.

The SAC utilizes a contextual teaching and learning method, which connects the content that students are learning (e.g., environmental science) with the context in which that content can be used (e.g., designing a city park and planting trees) and also with attributions of the self in real-world situations—attributions of the self such as self-efficacy, which can be learned through a project-based learning activity. A student can learn that she has a belief that she can accomplish this project as a member of a student group, and that she has a new set of personal beliefs that the environment is important to her. Finally, she discovers that creating new sustainable methods is her true calling professionally, so as to save the planet from global warming.

SAC is a flexible pedagogy that requires teachers to creatively identify and incorporate as many of the iSelf self-system and positive psychology attributes as possible to provide personalized learning opportunities.

Connecting Academic Content to the Self

Connecting content with context is an important component part of bringing meaning to the learning process and making learning more personalized. Further, SAC's intent is to access the natural learning system that all students possess—learning about one's self—as this is one's first interest.

The self-schema component of the iSelf model is critical to learning and growing and developing as a person through academic courses and all learning environments, and it is important for teachers, parents, and counselors, and all those committed to student well-being, to use it in their work. Leading self-referential scholars underscore this view: "In order for self-reference to be such a useful encoding process, the self must be a uniform, well-structured concept. During the recall phase of the study, subjects probably use the self as a retrieval cue" (Moscovitch and Craik, 1976). "In order for [self-reference] to be functional, the self must be a consistent and uniform schema" (Rogers, Kuiper, and Kirker, 1977, p. 686).

In two experiments, incidental recall of rated words indicated that adjectives rated under the self-reference task were recalled the best. These results indicate that self-reference is a rich and powerful encoding process. As an aspect of the human information-processing system, the self appears to function as a superordinate schema that is deeply involved in the processing, interpretation, and memory of personal information (Rogers, Kuiper, and Kirker, 1977, p. 677).

In addition to motivating a student's engagement in deeper learning instructional practices, positive academic mind-sets can also be seen as important deeper learning outcomes. The outcomes of academic programs are not only content knowledge and academic competencies, but also the people that students become from having participated in their educational experiences. To develop young people with a positive and efficacious sense of self and confidence in their abilities to engage with and contribute to the world, schools need to provide deeper learning opportunities in which students can follow their interests, strengthen bonds with peers, collaborate with a diverse range of people, build their competence over time, and come to see that accomplishment is built upon sustained hard work (Farrington, 2013).

Healing Childhood Trauma with SAC

Children are under stress to perform, to meet specific learning standards through their schooling. We disregard children's socioemotional needs and excessively highlight their intellectual growth and demonstration of skills or competencies, creating a chilling environment that contributes to bullying behaviors and victimization.

A student of coauthor Henry finishing up her M.Ed. degree, "Cassie," was assigned to a 3rd-grade public school classroom to observe children who were learning how to read and to assist when needed. One of Cassie's students, "Michael," had scored low on the Dynamic Indicators of Basic Early Literacy (DIBELS) assessment used extensively in elementary schools to measure reading fluency—this test measures the rate and accuracy of reading. Rate of reading is a count of the number of words read within a given time span, and accuracy is the ability to read a word aloud that matches the print on the page. The tests measure reading fluency as though it can be converted to a simple "hit" or "miss" measure. Words read correctly are "hits" and an error is a "miss;" the more times a child can hit the right word in one or two minutes, the better the child's fluency scores are (AIMS web training, 2004).

A skilled educator is trained to use these assessments and data derived from these for use in data-driven instruction. This means that if Michael scored low, where the number of misses in a minute is high, then a reading intervention and associated strategy is used to boost the DIBELS scores. The lead classroom teacher was upset with Michael and declared that he could not read and needed special remediation.

Upon observing Michael's emotional upset and sense that he had been defeated, Cassie took it upon herself to take Michael into a quiet corner of the classroom and read the book *Frog and Toad Together* (Lobel, 1983) with him. Cassie observed that Michael could read and, more important, understand and comprehend what he was reading—just not quite as fast as is required for DIBELS and for early childhood educators feeling the stress to improve reading scores.

Did Michael's teacher really know him? The reading material required for assessment was detached from the reader's experience of the story, words, and meanings—and from the whole child who was reading. When Cassie read with Michael, the material became more pertinent and personal, with a more meaningful and direct transfer of content to Michael's personal experience. Therefore, this produced better literacy results as well as less stress, anxiety, and potential harm to Michael's sense of self-belief system that he was a good person and could read.

How does this case relate to increased incidences of bullying in our education system? In all a child's primary cultural learning sources (schooling among them), learning is detached and decontextualized from the learner, from the whole child's mind, body, and soul. When learning becomes solely about acquiring content and is not related to the child's own experiences or emotional responses and relevant development potential, then the child feels that he is objectified—that he is somehow less important than the number of hits and misses in a minute.

In the context of Michael's classroom dynamics, as the class was moved ahead with other higher-level reading material, Michael felt bad about himself when he realized that he had not measured up to his teacher's expectations for DIBELS performance. He felt shamed in front of his classmates, his peer group. Cassie reported that Michael felt marginalized, separate from the group and therefore not belonging. He was questioning himself as a competent learner and, more directly, as a good person; the seeds of fear and self-doubt were planted.

The classroom is where children of all ages and abilities learn to construct or create a self, a mind, and brain. Michael will automatically respond emotionally to these circumstances, either positively or negatively. This visceral effect will impact his learning pathways and his ability to develop a mind that is comfortable and motivated to learn both interpsychological and intrapsychological. Without his teacher or parents helping him interpret these learning and socioemotional experiences in a way that enables a positive self-construct, he will become frustrated and react emotionally. Michael may become angry, wanting to demonstrate to himself and his classmates that he has some abilities. To cover up his shame in not being as able as his peers, he could find another way to demonstrate efficacy and regain his footing with his classmates, as a pathway to feel good about himself.

This scenario is replayed over and over again in classrooms throughout the United States, whenever children have difficulty meeting the expectations of their teachers, parents, or classmates. Our children do not have the mental mind-set or psychological paradigm with which to process and understand these omnipresent stressors. They have not been taught how to construct a self, a healthy self, which consists of self-concept, identity, purpose and dreams in life, and emotional intelligence, among other iSelf attributions. Because the vast majority of children are fundamentally good people and aspire to be good to their highest potentials, they become upset when they do not measure up to external expectations; they often want to act out with aggressive behaviors. The more they feel the effectiveness of treating others badly because they themselves feel bad, the more this becomes a cycle of learned reactions and behavior that defines who they are. We are not allowing our children to be children, to develop without forcing them to learn information that is so separate from their own experiences and such a far transfer from their realities.

Michael could, on the other hand, retreat into silence, withdraw, and isolate himself from the stressors and external forces as a natural defense mechanism. If the circumstances are too much for his psyche to be able to handle, he will learn how to cope through dissociation, a clinical term meaning that the mind separates or detaches feelings and emotions from the circumstances in his life experience, especially specific experiences that threaten his sense of self. This is called "adaptive dissociation." This leads to one of numerous dissociative disorders, including dissociative identity disorder and depersonalization disorder, among others. According to a recent updated study with recommendations for the updated DSM-IV manual, dissociation is a disruption of and/or discontinuity in the normal, subjective integration of one or more aspects of psychological functioning, including—but not limited to—memory, identity, consciousness, perception, and motor control. In essence, aspects of psychobiological functioning that should be associated, coordinated, and/or linked are not (Spiegel et al., 2011, p. 826).

We can see, then, how Michael's psychobiological functioning between identity and consciousness most likely could result in a dissociative state, which could produce an unawareness of either bullying or withdrawal behaviors. Dissociative disorders rob children of happy, healthy development. So many children are in a constant state of anxiety or trauma because they do not have the mind-set or psychological tools to process and understand modern life.

We know that motivation and enjoyment are critical to learning to read and to all learning, and the child who enjoys reading (and learning) is likely to read on his own and will gain the practice necessary to become a lifelong, skilled reader (Fox, 2008). Michael's case provides an example. If we teach literacy, then we can also simultaneously teach positive emotions and identity through learning to read. If teachers focus on personalized learning and the cultivation of love for learning, they are in fact critical protective factors in the lives of children, adolescents, and young adults.

Recommendations for Teachers

These recommendations also appear in the Integrated Self Model section and are relevant to SAC.

Teachers can strengthen their students' self-knowledge and well-being in both simple and complex ways. Teachers can make a significant difference by developing programs for students, working with each other across units, and reaching up through the hierarchies of leadership for school-wide change. Teachers can:

- Read the iSelf distinctions and incorporate at least one distinction into an assignment, noting for students when they have strengthened their awareness of the distinction. For example, self-efficacy can be demonstrated by defending a mathematical theorem, and locus of control can be demonstrated by student taking responsibility for the school's recycling program.
- Explore ways to incorporate emotional learning in cognitive assignments, such as connecting assignments to making a meaningful contribution to the community that students are passionate about.
- Form a teacher group to explore ways to encourage and recognize students' self-knowledge and self-responsibility.
- Hold intra- and interdepartmental discussions on the promising and high-impact practices in this *Toolkit* to explore ones to incorporate into classes and school activities.

- Develop preventative programming based on the iSelf model's self-system and positive psychology attributions.
- Create new student handbooks and other resources.
- Build the iSelf attributes into home-room programs.
- Develop programs that support students' developmental progress towards their personal, college and professional goals.
- Design metrics to measure students' well-being.
- Hold teacher professional development sessions on the many ways to impart well-being and self-knowledge using the *Mental Health for All Toolkit*, through PLCs or in-service sessions.
- Make presentations to school leaders and community members on the iSelf distinctions they feel are most important to include in the school's mission and programs.

Further, teachers can work across grade levels and administrative functions to initiate school-wide systems of support for mental health and wellness. Schools should bring together representatives from mental health, counseling, and teaching functions and other leaders to:

- Develop a new mission statement that puts well-being at the center of the school.
- Develop a school-wide plan for tangible and integrated programs that deliver on the promise of the well-being mission.
- Determine school-wide themes to engage students in making a difference in society.
- Design metrics to measure how the new well-being mission is helping to achieve school goals.
- Work with information technology professionals to develop online systems for students to self-manage their goals, competencies, and accomplishments.
- Redesign school programs to include the values of well-being, self-knowledge, and societal contribution.

Examples for Teachers

What is common among these examples from K–12 classrooms is that each of the teachers was able to impart iSelf attributes through everyday lessons and activities, thereby placing their student's interests, emotional and psychological well-being, as well as a sense of fun, creativity, leadership, and responsibility at the center of their teaching. They personalized the learning for each of their students using iSelf distinctions with dramatic results.

Example 1: "Learning Literacy through the Self: Learning the Self through Literacy"

Here is a sample lesson plan for preservice and in-service master teachers and seasoned counselors that teaches how to include self-understanding in the classroom.

Lesson Goals

This lesson introduces the central issues in development of the self through literacy and learning literacy through the self during the early childhood stage of human development. (Students will be asked to use our class discussion and presentation in class and Ormond [2011] text chapters 9, 10, 12, and 13 as references.) Students will develop and demonstrate an ability to teach literacy concepts and empower self-understanding through a developmentally appropriate lesson activity.

Resources

Students will be asked to draw upon chapters 9, 10, 12, and 13 in the Ormond (2011) text; a handout titled "Acquiring Literacy Skills That Have a Purpose and Deal with Real-Life Experiences" (Newman, Copple, & Bredekamp, 1998); the children's book they chose and used for their literacy connection project (another assignment during this course); and the "Learning Literacy Through Meaning" video on demand available on our course webpage link and at the Annenberg Learner website (http://www.learner.org/resources/browse.html#FL).

Methods/Representations of Learning

Each student or student pair will be asked to prepare one lesson activity that would take approximately 20 to 30 minutes to deliver to a class of elementary school 3rd graders:

1. Lesson activity will develop three distinctions of self discussed in class and described in text: self-concept, self-esteem, and self-efficacy.
2. Lesson activity will help the student assess and develop at least one attribute in each of the three developmental domains: socioemotional, physical, and cognitive development, from early childhood to late adolescence and early adulthood.
3. Lesson activity will develop these literacy skills: phonemic awareness, phonological awareness, and semantic cues.
4. Lesson activity will be of professional educator quality, suitable for inclusion into professional teaching portfolios.

Analysis of Lesson

This lesson produced numerous outstanding lesson plans by preservice teachers who went on to become certified as early childhood, middle school, and special education teachers. Many used their lesson plans proudly, as exemplars of excellence in their professional portfolios.

Example 2: Lesson Plan—"Features of a Civilization"

Teachers in coauthor Henry's graduate level education courses have taken the SAC processes and developed lesson plans and learning activities for their classrooms. This example demonstrates how the SAC can be implemented in high school social studies. This 9th-grade social studies lesson was developed by a new teacher with fewer than 3 years' experience teaching (used with permission).

Duration

Three class periods

Lesson Goals

This lesson teaches students a broader view of themselves and their potential contributions to the world by connecting book concepts to real-world problems. It also imparts social studies content standards on civics and government and empowers students to develop a self-concept, creativity or critical thinking, feelings of love and belonging to a group, self-efficacy, locus of control, and purpose in life through teaching content standards.

Resources

Students will participate in in-class presentations and whole-class discussion. Teacher will provide writing and discussion prompts for students to use in group discussions.

Activity/Representations of Learning

1. Create student teams made up of four to six students. In group discussion, students should rank the importance of different features of civilization.
2. During these discussions, students should be encouraged to express passion about their views and discuss, argue, and debate with respect and consideration for other viewpoints. These discussions should defend why the group ranked features in a particular order. Through this discussion, students will develop a deeper understanding of their purpose in life, their values, and possibly interests that would lead them to their future careers.

3. Lesson activity will help you assess and develop at least one attribute in each of the three developmental domains: socioemotional, physical, and cognitive development.
4. The following questions will prompt a follow-up discussion:
   a. What did the students find difficult or challenging about ranking the features of a civilization in order of importance?
   b. What were some issues each group faced when doing this activity?
   c. What were the reactions to seeing/hearing other groups' rankings, and how did they compare across the groups?
   d. Do the students think there is a "correct" answer to the ranking? Why or why not?

Analysis of Lesson

The teacher who designed this lesson reported that students did a great job of using and developing iSelf components developed through this portion of the lesson: self-efficacy, through developing their beliefs about their own views, and purpose in life, values, and self-determination, as students felt a greater sense of belonging, feeling they were in control of their views and direction of discussions and gaining competence in formulating their own beliefs and arguing for them.

Other important civilization features, like those in our constitution, serve to deepen not only social studies standards content knowledge but also the relationship between personal attributions and our constitution (e.g., pursuit of happiness and equality). Happiness is a positive psychology attribute; equality indicates meaning in life, and both are explored through this activity.

At the beginning of each lesson, the teacher utilizes a writing prompt, or bell ringer exercise, to support students in connecting with prior learning and deepen personal meanings from the content.

History Journal Prompt 1 (Day Three Lesson)

Which feature of a civilization do you think is most important to the success/functionality of the civilization as a whole? Which feature of a civilization do you think is least important? Explain why.

Alternatively, if you are having difficulty with this, you may instead reflect on the role of a couple of the features or comment on our discussion about the role of government in our society: what it should be versus what it is.

Analysis of Journal Prompt

Several iSelf components were developed through this portion of the lesson; students related the features of civilization back to these iSelf distinction/attributes to find meaning in life. One student wrote an essay response that created a new civilization based on the feature of "justice," calling it "Justice-ism" and describing what that civilization would be like to live in. The teacher then also referenced how this is the basis for self-concept: having a future dream to create a world that reflects this feature, maybe through law or advocacy. The teacher imparted purpose and direction to a student's life through the lesson by referencing iSelf distinctions in this way. The teacher also reported that students were able to relate the bigger ideas explored in the lesson to the real world by asking "why" questions.

The Self-Referential Method Used in a Social Studies Lesson

The SAC uses a self-referential method to help impart iSelf attributions through lessons. Applying the iSelf model to this "Features of a Civilization" lesson, or any lesson, is really as simple and as straightforward as developing any lesson using a three-stage, "backward" planning method.

Think through what self-system and positive psychology attributes you would like to impart in a particular lesson in the same way you choose academic content standards from your district's supplied list (or one that is supplied for you by your state's Department of Education or National Council for the Social Studies Standards [http://www.socialstudies.org] or Common Core standards). Just as you review the content standards, review the iSelf attributes that you feel you could impart, either because of your commitment to imparting these or because they lend themselves to a particular lesson and meet the personalized needs of your students.

For example, in the civilizations lesson previously described, you can help students gain a self-concept and meaning in life, just to mention two. To illustrate, when you ask which features of a civilization are the most and least important, you can relate this question back to the iSelf attribute of "life meaning."

List those self-attributes that you will assess, either formatively or summatively, as evidence. Be precise in what you are looking for and how you will assess: worksheets, essays, participation in discussions, and so on. Throughout, when delivering the lesson, describe what specific iSelf attributes you hope to impart.

Students could write an essay response about creating a new civilization based on a feature they admire, such as "justice," and then describe what life would be like in that civilization for the student, her close family members, her friends, and the world at large. The self-referential ("self–other–all") approach helps students connect more deeply with the content and can go so far as to potentially inspire them to a future career.

As with any method, the more you practice, the greater facility you will gain. We would strongly suggest attempting to apply the self-theory attributes in all your lessons. Incorporate iSelf attributes directly into your formal lesson plan, and see what works and what does not. As with any lesson, some things work better than others.

You will also find that you have a particular motivation to impart one or a set of self-distinctions—perhaps meaning in life, or self-concept, or self-esteem—whereas others are not that important to you immediately. The point being, try different ones and see what works!

Example 3: Lesson Plan—"Energy Conservation Is All Around Us!"

This 6th-grade science lesson was developed by a master teacher with 10 years of experience teaching (used with permission).

Lesson Duration

Five class periods

Lesson Essential Questions

- How can I use resources more responsibly? (self)
- How can I teach my family to save energy? (other)
- How can I make a difference in the world? (all)
- What do students need to learn to be able to answer these essential questions?
- Assessment prompt 1: Many of us waste a lot of energy and resources each day.
- Assessment prompt 2: By changing behaviors and materials, we can make a big difference.
- Assessment prompt 3: Every person has the ability and the responsibility to take action regarding saving energy and resources.

Activating Strategy

Students will draw a picture of a place (e.g., bedroom, kitchen, store, classroom) and label all the items that use energy. Here are the key vocabulary terms:

- Renewable resources
- Nonrenewable resources

- Wind energy
- Hydroelectric
- Geothermal
- Solar energy
- Conservation
- Energy efficiency
- Fossil fuels

Teaching Strategies

- Graphic organizer
- Vocabulary matrix
- Cause-and-effect fishbone
- Self-referential (self–other–all)
- Concentric circles (diagram and worksheet)

Instruction

- Guest speakers launch lesson
- Students apply knowledge at home with take-home kits
- Students calculate how much energy and money they have saved as individuals, within their families, and as a class
- Many summarizing strategies are applied throughout lesson
- Students use their book to learn ways that energy is being wasted and how they can conserve

Assignments and Assessments

- Vocabulary acrostic. Students create vocabulary acrostics to summarize what they've learned about a given word or concept; they share these with the class.
- Vocabulary matrix. Students complete a matrix to learn vocabulary words; the matrix has four columns: word, definition, example, and picture.
- Cause-and-effect fishbone. Students show how things they do can have a direct effect on helping themselves, their families, and the world.
- Concentric circles. Students use concentric circles to answer the following questions: How does saving energy help me? How can I help my family? How can I make a difference in the world?

Extending Thinking Activity

- The energy-saving concentric circles graphic organizer demonstrates the integration of concepts.

Analysis of Lesson

Note that the teacher who designed this lesson placed the "self–other–all" approach in the essential questions and discussed these with the class. This alone got their attention. In the environmental sciences lesson, the teacher observed that one student, Daniel, demonstrated self-efficacy and leadership and new levels of engagement and motivation. The teacher asked the class three essential questions demonstrating the self-referential teaching method:

1. How can I use resources more responsibly (applying what is learned to self)?
2. How can I teach my family to save energy (applying what I have learned to others)?
3. How can I make a difference in the world (applying what is learned to all)?

Daniel, in response to these questions, immediately took charge of the classroom and the learning; he organized the entire class into groups and assigned jobs. The lead classroom teacher reflected that she was literally stunned to see Daniel so energetic, dynamic, proactive, and positive when he had previously been a polite, quiet, and reserved student.

Daniel wrote a newsletter that solicited input from all his classmates on researched data about recycling in their community, the entire nation, and potential problems and solutions. Please keep in mind that Daniel was only in the 6th grade! He organized a school-wide recycling program and invited all classrooms to participate, and all did—100% involvement. He sent home copies of a letter to parents to participate in recycling in their homes with their children. He earned the highest grade in the class on all criteria in the teacher's rubric. Prior to this, he was a somewhat withdrawn student, seemingly going through the motions in every class activity. Daniel had always been a talented student academically but was not using his intelligence to his full potential. Through applying the self–other–all and self-referential methods to his own learning, he discovered through his own experience numerous self-theory and positive psychology concepts that empowered him to achieve academically and develop important personal qualities, such as leadership and self-expression.

Middle School Homework

This same teacher spent 10 minutes one morning talking about "intrinsic motivation" to her class. Up until this conversation, her students had difficulty getting homework done on time and at a high quality. That very same day, 90% of her students had their homework completed prior to leaving for the day, with the remaining 10% bringing it into class the next day. This had never happened in this class—or in any other class she had taught in her 10 years of experience.

Recommendations for Parents

In order to shift a child's way of being from very anxious and nervous to experiencing more inner peace, presence and joy, parents should acknowledge when key lifelong personal skills are developing. These could include recognizing grit and the associated sense of higher purpose in life; this instills a new self-confidence and self-esteem.

Also, as was previously described in the Integrated Self Model section, for parents we recommend referencing one or more of the 30 iSelf model distinctions when communicating with your children. Acknowledging your child's grit or resilience is an example of commitment toward something deemed important by your child. Or, when your child is emoting about something seems unimportant to you, acknowledge their abilities to feel—the iSelf attribution "affect"—and ask what this means. Develop a family mission statement that puts mental health and well-being at the core of family relationships and activities. Determine family rules than ensure technology use supports the family mission rather than detracts from it. Communicate your family mission to your children's teachers so they can better support your children during the school day.

Parents may also choose to enroll their children into extracurricular courses on self-awareness and life purpose and direction.

Example for Parents: The Champions Program— "We Develop Champions in Life!"

The Brzycki Group & The Center for the Self in Schools offers The Champions Program, a curriculum that incorporates the Integrated Self Model. We believe that children in today's world want to live a life aspiring to a higher standard of excellence, mental health, and wellness, to a better life and a better world. Children are requesting from us the opportunity to build a life and a world with a new value system, one based upon personal character, personal well-being, self-understanding, and high self-esteem.

Since 1986, we have been proud to make available to these high minded children of the world an impactful educational program that helps them manifest the life of their dreams, one based upon total well-being, personal discovery, and taking charge of manifesting their own destinies in life. We have listened to their requests for these new tools with which to build a better life, and responded with a unique and innovative program called The Champions Program.

The Champions Program is a curriculum of empowerment solidly grounded in the principles of human development, psychology of well-being, educational psychology, and educational philosophy. Throughout the program, students strengthen cognitive and metacognitive development, self-determination, contextual awareness, and sensory processing skills.

The Champions Program empowers what is possible in the young person versus focusing upon problems to fix. We assume that the young person is on a unique path of personal discovery to create his or her own destiny, and wants to live a life of total health, wholeness, and accomplishment.

Your son or daughter will learn how to create his or her own paradigm of self, self-understanding, self-esteem, and character to dramatically impact the quality of your child's life. Your child will take away a powerful system of learning that empowers the understanding and expression of his or her own unique potential—it is a tool that will stay with your child forever.

Results Produced

Champions' participants typically experience these results (these are not presented as future promises or expectations, but as reference points to consider):

1. Experience a shift in their way of being in the world, more at ease and less anxious
2. Learn contextual awareness and build their sensory processing skills

3. Learn to create the life that they really want, not merely because something is a good idea

4. Are able to set clear goals and develop effective strategies to achieve them

5. Take full responsibility for the quality of their life; they stop blaming others for their circumstances

6. Are able to handle change, upset, and transitions with skill and ease

7. Experience a new level of authentic self-expression

8. Take ownership for the results of their projects, because they learn the importance of choice

9. Learn their unique learning styles and how to best employ newly discovered talents

10. Strengthen their sense of self agency and locus of control

11. Enhance their executive control

12. Improve organizational skills

13. Improve relationships with family and friends and heighten their social understanding and awareness

14. Increase their excitement about learning and learning about health and well-being

15. Follow-up by a results management team, made up of parents, teachers, Champions course teachers, coaches, relatives, and others, reinforcing the importance of building self-esteem and self-knowledge through accomplishments

16. Harness their own high standards of excellence in school and home and self

17. Learn to reframe "failures" as steps toward a goal

18. Learn to produce results that are aligned with their own sense of purpose and vision

19. Learn to take responsibility for their own emotional, physical, psychological, and spiritual well-being

20. Learn how to enjoy the challenges inherent in taking on initiative

21. Are happy, fully alive, and turned on to life

22. Learn the joy and satisfaction in practicing personal discipline

23. Learn that they are powerful and make a positive difference

24. Achieve new levels of accomplishment

25. Exercise leadership

26. Value their unique voice, style, and talents

27. Participate actively in groups

Recommendations for Students

These recommendations were included in the Integrated Self Model section as well. Individual students and student groups, especially those in the higher grade levels in high school, do not need to wait for their school or families to make systemic changes in order to put well-being and self-knowledge at the center of their own learning experiences. Students can:

- Read and learn more about the iSelf distinctions, and provide themselves with a new awareness of the self-system and positive psychology attributions that have been shown to lead to positive life trajectories.
- Complete the Success Predictor described in the last section of the *Toolkit* to proactively develop a structure in their schools and families to accomplish their goals and pursue their dreams.
- Develop peer-to-peer counseling groups to discuss the iSelf distinctions and encourage self-authorship.
- Reach out to teachers to engage in extracurricular and community-based projects.
- Create groups to meet with school leaders to discuss needs and request resources to support their well-being.
- Continue to voice that the purpose of education is well-being for self, family, friends, institutions, and society.

Example for Students: The Vision Course for Adolescents

Students may also ask their parents to enroll them into extracurricular courses on self-awareness and life purpose and direction. The Brzycki Group & The Center for the Self in Schools offers The Vision Course.

The Vision Course is impactful, results driven, and profound. You bring to the course those issues and concerns that are important to the quality of your life. The course is designed around your particular future dreams—personal, school, relationships, and family. The Vision Course is powerful because you are. We challenge you to design your own destiny for your life!

It is during the 8 weeks of The Vision Course that you learn the tools to design your own greatness, your own success, your own destiny. In the course you learn to develop your own understanding of yourself and your life, and then to recontextualize them toward a new perspective about your future—one based upon your dreams of what you see is possible.

You will learn what your life is all about, what is important to you, what is your unique purpose in life, and tap into a new, inner motivation to see and achieve your greatness. You will learn that your life is about knowing you and about being related to possibilities bigger than yourself and about knowing that you can make them happen. In this course you are in charge of your own learning, and you fully utilize those resources—inner character and innate talents and abilities—that are available to you to achieve what you want. You will create distinctions about yourself that empower your greatness and the full manifestation of your vision.

This course is usually delivered during the summer months or during the school year in an after school setting or on the weekends.

Toolkit High Impact Practice— Success Predictor (SP)

The Success Predictor is a highly effective tool used by teachers, parents, and school counselors to help guide young people of all ages, developmental stages and levels, and walks of life toward their highest expressions of what is possible for them. It is used to assess, diagnose, and intervene into the mind-set of students who want to see and achieve their full and unique potentials life—empowering them to succeed and manifest their full and unique potentials!

The Success Predictor is a framework for personal development, to help students determine who they are and those pathways that will lead to their definition of success. The Success Predictor is typically used to: determine internal motivations to succeed, understand reference points of capabilities, diagnose internal states of well-being, formulate career aspirations, understand academic program interests, guide college selection and fit, guide life and career directions, understand personal paradigms of reality, guide interventions, among others. The Success Predictor is used to help guide you from making a transformation from the person you think you are supposed to be, to that which you know you are meant to be.

From a child's, adolescent's, or young adult's perspective, learning about who they are during their school and college years and how to create a great life generally with numerous possible experiences offers a special opportunity, most likely for the first time in their lives, to reflect upon "Who am I now?" and "How have my life circumstances shaped me to be the person I am supposed to be?" These circumstances may be family values, childhood trauma(s), traditions, behaviors, and dominant cultural forces (such as social media, prevalence of prescription drugs, mass school shootings, and global warming, among others). Students can reflect on "Who am I meant to be, now that I am on my own?" The opportunity to consider life purpose is special and unique. "Do I have a calling in life, repressed dreams for my life?" and "What is meaningful to me?" are among the important questions to ask at different developmental stages.

How the Success Predictor Works

Emotions are important because they motivate us to grow and develop and make a difference in the world—the real world. Without emotions and motivated reasoning, change is not possible. When a student knows what she wants, and she is passionate about it for whatever reason, structural tension is created. Structural tension is a clinical term to describe the energy created when an individual concurrently envisions a desired future state, while being completely aware of the limitations of present or current reality. The difference between the desired future state and current reality creates a tension that seeks resolution toward one or the other. The idea of structural tension applies the first axiom of structural dynamics (Odum, 1988) to individual change. In any counseling or teaching relationship, it is critical to establish this structural tension in order to empower positive change. When this tension is created, emotional thought drives the change process. As teachers, parents, and counselors, it is our responsibility to guide positive changes and provide tools or methods so that students can learn how to do this for themselves.

The Success Predictor uses the first axiom of structural dynamics (Odum, 1988) that tension seeks resolution (Figure 3). This initiates the change process—the emotional desire to attain a future state, a goal, a dream. This axiom is essential for all to understand and apply to their lives and careers.

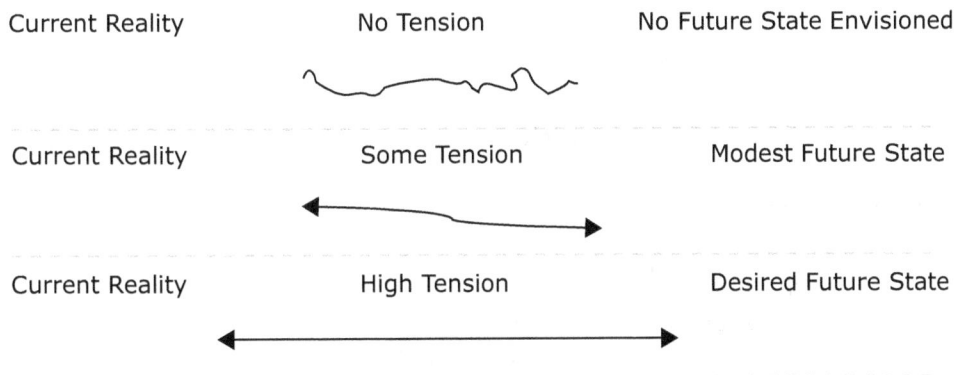

Current Reality	No Tension	No Future State Envisioned
Current Reality	Some Tension	Modest Future State
Current Reality	High Tension	Desired Future State

Figure 3. Structural Tension in the Success Predictor

Figure 3 presents three levels of tension between the left side, current reality, and the right side, the degree to which a future state is desired. The first level is "No Tension," which indicates that a person is just going through the motions, floating through life, allowing circumstances to dictate direction and feelings, and sense of self, with very little commitment toward anyone or anything, including self and personal growth and development. Additionally, the person does not have a clear picture of present reality, either emotional states or physical situation.

The second level, "Moderate Tension," indicates a modest commitment to a desired future state, most often with the ability to envision general circumstances such as more money, a new car, or better relationships. Most likely this person is not able to envision a future state that includes emotions or to feel as an important part of the quality of life. This person is also not very clear about his or her present emotional state.

The third level, "High Tension," indicates the ability to dream about a complete and whole picture that includes emotional states of being, who one wants to become (e.g., a good person who makes a difference), and numerous and clear distinctions about both emotional and circumstantial future realities. This person also clearly identifies current emotional states, even if they include sadness or frustration that the future state is yet to be realized. This person also is clearer about unique potential in life—something special that he or she has to give or contribute to others.

Helping students understand who they are and their own pathways to success in K-12 schooling, college, and later in life happens through effective counseling and teaching through workshops that changes minds and brains in the same way and through the same pathway—the integrated self of the person in our care. In workshop settings, we are changing behaviors through changing thoughts and feelings that impact the neural networks in our brains.

When a student is learning, all these are at work; all are changing simultaneously. As such, as counselors and teachers, we need to be aware of and responsible for our interventions, as they are impacting the self of the students at deep, fundamental levels.

Students already know that they want something, to be a better person, to be successful, to change the world in their unique manner. They have self-interest in attending a workshop and attempting new activities, such as playing musical instruments or participating in sports. Teachers, parents, and counselors need to be aware that students have a natural internal drive, or intrinsic motivations, fueled by emotions.

We draw upon the breakthrough work in mind, brain, and education (MBE) for a deeper look into students' inner dynamics: "The processes of recognizing and responding to complex situations, which we suggest hold the origins of creativity, are fundamentally emotional and social. As such, they are shaped by and evaluated within a cultural context and are based upon emotional processing. No matter how complex and esoteric they become, our repertoire of behavioral and cognitive options continues to exist in the service of emotional goals" (Immordino-Yang and

Damasio, 2007, p. 7). In sum, everything we do for ourselves or for others serves the self at some or many levels.

It is the self of the individual that engages in learning experiences that marry emotions with thinking to arrive at an outcome, a result from the learning experience. All learning is dedicated toward achieving goals that emphasize the personal and social domains. The self mediates between the social and the personal, and the external with the internal. We make conscious decisions to place ourselves in particular situations where we are called upon to learn, to express, and to add to the interactive dynamics of the interpsychological and intrapsychological processes required to succeed or manifest our goal. Damasio's "collection of systems dedicated to goal-oriented thinking" reinforces the view that reasoning toward the manifestation of a dream considers both personal and social interests, not an either/or perspective. Said another way, inherently, at the "being" level as human beings, we strive to produce positive outcomes for both ourselves and others.

Directions for How to Apply the Success Predictor to Your Personal Situation

Inquire into a new possibility and what is possible for you in your life:

1. Why is constructivism and positive psychology important for people to study and apply?
2. How does a student actually "construct" a self?
3. In which ways does a person's level of consciousness impact the ability to construct knowledge about one's self?
4. What is the DNA of consciousness and is it important?
5. Is the degree to which a student/person can construct a self-concept and a self-system important to academic learning excellence, life satisfaction, well-being?

Quotes to Support Your Inquiry

"Dream up a good life!"

—Jim Carrey

"Some men see things as they are and say why. I dream things that never were and say, why not?"

—Robert F. Kennedy

"To both Piaget and Erikson, the person does not become a true individual or personality until he has integrated his thoughts and feelings about himself into a total life perspective which expands beyond personal interest to the whole of mankind."

—David Elkind, from *Six Psychological Studies*, by Jean Piaget

"Subject-object theory brings together two powerful lines of intellectual discourse that have influenced not only the field of psychology but nearly every corner of intellectual life in the West in this century. These two lines of thought are constructivism, the idea that people or systems constitute or construct reality; and developmentalism, the idea that people or organic systems evolve through qualitatively different eras of increasing complexity according to regular principles of stability and change."

—Robert Kegan, from *In Over Our Heads*

Step-by-Step Instructions

The Success Predictor is a questionnaire for you to complete that will help guide you towards what is next—through personal, school and life transitions. The questionnaire will help you to understand the important connections among personal life purpose and dreams, academic interests and academic program selection, career aspirations, and future directions.

Please review the following pages and become familiar with the word definitions or categories used in the Success Predictor model. Also, become familiar with the questions posed within each word category. Word definitions are provided as well as questions that assist you in formulating a personal connection to the word category. For purposes of completing the Success Predictor questionnaire, each word category is a level of your consciousness, your own knowing about you and the way you frame your reality. Therefore, it is important that you take each word category and develop a personal experience of it, or derive personal meaning.

Please take the 10 word distinctions or categories and view them as a hierarchy or levels of understanding. The 10 word distinctions below are not ordered by level; therefore, please organize them by level, much like solving a puzzle, which assists in the transformation of how you organize your own view of reality and self. You may need to make a number of attempts to organize the distinctions to solve the puzzle. There is no absolute correct puzzle solution, but there is a best solution that most accurately represents a hierarchy of consciousness.

Levels of understanding means that the category "purpose" requires a higher level of understanding or broader view than the category "plans" does, as one example. Therefore, when formulating your response to the category "purpose," please consider your level of understanding and view. Remember, when you have completed the questionnaire, you will have a snapshot or present picture of who you are and your view of your reality, self, and future success, so please consider your responses carefully and consciously.

When completing the questionnaire, feel free to use internet images, pictures cut out of magazines, or photos from your life, and paste them into the blank pages provided for each category or on additional pages (these pages with pictures form your personal "dream journal"). These pictures assist in clarifying what each level of understanding looks like and feels like to you.

Your responses in each category may be in written and/or picture cut-out form.

The Success Predictor has 10 categories (listed in no particular order):

Results. Evidence that you are on the right track toward manifesting your purpose, vision, goals, and plans; a compass; what occurs after you take action.

Mission. An inner calling to pursue an activity or perform a service; a vocation; the area of life where one will manifest their life's purpose.

Commitments. What you are determined to do; a pledge to do something; a state of being bound emotionally or intellectually to someone or something, like a strong belief.

Being. The essence of a human being; the totality of all things that exist; the qualities that constitute existence or essence; one's basic nature.

Tactics. Step-by-step actions to take to implement your plans; a series of steps toward achieving a goal or implementing a plan.

Goals. To accomplish something by a certain time; "what by when."

Vision. What you can see in the future, a dream of what is possible; a mental image produced by the imagination, to see in your mind's eye; unusual competence or perception; intelligent foresight.

Strategies. An approach to take, or a method to use to accomplish a specific goal; how you will manifest your goals; approaches or alternatives.

Plans. To form a scheme or program for the accomplishment of a goal; to make a graphic representation, like a blueprint; how you will execute the strategies formulated.

Purpose. The reason why you are here, for your existence; raison d'être; describes or includes your basic nature or being.

Notes: (1) When completing your responses to these categories, please use as much space as required, or as many pages as you want; (2) Brief descriptions and examples are provided in each category to assist you in formulating your own understandings. (3) Source of definitions: The American Heritage College Dictionary, Third Edition.

PAUSE HERE: Please do not go the next section of the Success Predictor until you have arranged the categories in a contextual hierarchy, and then confirmed your understanding with a teacher, parent, or counselor. The most accurate representation of the hierarchy is found at the end of this chapter.

Please use this space (or additional pages) to make numerous attempts at organizing your understanding of the 10 categories into a contextual hierarchy.

The "Why" Contextual Levels of Understanding

Purpose

Your purpose is the reason why you are here, in this life. It is what you commit your life to, something bigger than yourself, using your unique talents, values, and vision in the service of creating a better world. It is part of the underlying motivation and driving force that guides your actions and brings you fulfillment. Your purpose engages a lifelong process that you can continuously discover and improve upon, and compels you to make a difference in your life, the lives of others, and the condition of the world.

The following George Bernard Shaw quote characterizes the spirit of a person's purpose:

> This is the true joy in life, the being used for a purpose recognized by yourself as a mighty one; the being a force of nature instead of a feverish selfish little clod of ailments and grievances complaining that the world will not devote itself to making you happy. I want to be thoroughly used up when I die, for the harder I work the more I live. I rejoice in life for its own sake. Life is no "brief candle" to me. It is a sort of splendid torch which I have got hold of for the moment, and I want to make it burn as brightly as possible before handing it on to future generations. (Man and Superman, 1973)

As a student, you will want to understand your purpose in order to guide your personal development, mental health and well-being, academic studies, career direction, and the selection of colleges that can help you manifest the difference you would like to make in the world.

Helpful Hint: Here are some characteristics of an effective purpose statement:

1. Clear and concise; no longer than two to five sentences
2. Present tense (i.e., "I make a difference in everything that I do.")
3. Simple to understand and remember
4. Congruent with your values and visions
5. Includes who or what you positively impact
6. Refers to a lifelong process that can never be totally obtained or outlived
7. Can be realized with your effort
8. Compels you to act with passion, energy, and commitment
9. Is a unique expression of you
10. Is inspirational to you (and possibly to others)

My Purpose is:

Mission

When you have a mission in life, you feel an inner calling to pursue an activity or to perform a service for humankind. This is sometimes a gut feeling, your intuition speaking, and is important to listen to. Your mission represents the pathway you take to manifest your purpose in family, school, relationships, and activities.

Your mission is something you know you are meant to do in service of creating a better world. Along with your purpose, it is part of the underlying motivation and driving force that guides your actions and brings you fulfillment. One central question to ask in formulating your mission is "where" in the world you will manifest your life's purpose. Where is your calling needed by others? Here is an example of a mission statement: "I serve children by helping them feel emotional safety and healing, and make it easier for them to love one another as the leader of a school."

You will want to understand your mission so that it can guide your career direction, the selection of your academic area of study, and the selection of colleges that can train you professionally to help you reach those who need your calling. Knowing whom you want to positively impact, you will have the focus to design a college application strategy that communicates your self-understanding and the difference you would like to make in the world. Referencing the mission statement example above, a college-bound student would study adolescent psychology and education, and then begin to develop internships in educational settings.

Helpful Hint: Here are some characteristics of an effective mission statement:

1. Clear and concise; no longer than five to seven sentences.
2. Present tense (e.g. "I am a teacher of emotional healing through families and schools.")
3. Congruent with your purpose and visions
4. Includes "who" or "what" you positively impact, and "where" in the world you will make a difference
5. Speaks to your own understanding of your inner calling
6. Is meaningful to you
7. Is a unique expression of you

<u>My Mission is:</u>

The "What" Contextual Levels of Understanding

Vision

You can create your future. Many of us plod along day after day, living as if we are simply playing out roles in a play that is already written for us. That play has not been written. You must create it through a vision of your ideal future. Vision is the design of your own destiny in life; it is your dream of what you want your life to be.

A clear understanding of your vision answers two questions: "What will I be doing?" (activities) and "What will I feel like?" (energy). It is usually easy to imagine the activities and tasks you will be doing, and the success you will be enjoying from doing those tasks. It is sometimes more difficult to imagine your energy, what personal and relationship behaviors, attitudes, and character traits you will be living by in order to produce the results you want.

Your vision is what you see is possible for you, for the world, and for your contributions and accomplishments. When formulating a vision or dream, do not ask, "Is this realistic?"; for if you are creating your own destiny, you decide if your dreams become a reality or not.

You will want to understand your vision so that it can guide your life's choices—for example, career direction and the selection of colleges where you can begin to create your ideal future. In your college application, you can clearly communicate your self-understanding and your vision for a better life and world.

Helpful Hint: Here are some characteristics of an effective vision statement:

1. Present tense (e.g. "I am challenged every day in my work with children and energized by the contributions I know I am making to make certain that children do not suffer in the world.")
2. Includes specific action details rather than broad generalities (e.g. "I volunteer one night per week at the hospital," versus "I serve others.")
3. Combines both what you are doing (activity or task) and how you are feeling when doing it (energy)
4. Includes information about all aspects of your future: school, family, relationships, work, spiritual, social, physical, emotional, financial, others
5. Congruent with your values and life purpose
6. It should be something you really want, not something you should want.
7. Formulated by you, in fact created by you based upon your own inner sense of what is possible for you! Note, not your parents, siblings, or others in your life.

My Vision is
(Use written words, images, or pictures to represent your vision.)

Commitments

Commitment is the triumph of possibility over resignation, of creating your life's destiny versus having it determined for you by others. Your commitments empower you to step beyond what is comfortable or predicable, beyond the limits that you thought you had—toward a dynamic and challenging life of active contribution and self-expression. Your commitments are what you believe in, your ground, or stand.

Your commitment is what you have pledged to do, to take a stand for, for you, for the world, and for your contributions and accomplishments. When determining your set of commitments, do not ask, "Will my commitments help me become famous?" Your commitments represent your own deeply held beliefs, regardless of the affirmation of others.

As a student, you will want to understand your commitments so that they can express your beliefs clearly and communicate them to other people. For example, if you are planning on going to college to achieve your mission of teaching music, your beliefs should be expressed in every communication throughout your college application process, during interviews, writing essays, and sending thank you letters.

Helpful Hint: Here are some characteristics of an effective commitment statement:

1. Present tense (e.g. "I am committed to making my purpose manifest in the world.")
2. Includes specific belief details rather than broad generalities (e.g. "I believe in the power of music to transform people's experiences of goodness in the world," versus "I love music.")
3. Includes information about all aspects of your future: school, family, relationships, work, spiritual, social, physical, emotional, financial, others
4. Congruent with your values and life purpose, and life dreams
5. Your commitments are your own, not derived from others.

<u>I am Committed to:</u>

Goals

Many of us think that our goals are our dreams. When we asked a student what were his dreams for his life, he answered with much confidence, "My dream is to go to college!" But very shortly thereafter, he said with more uncertainty, "I guess that is a goal and not a dream. I guess I really don't know what my dreams are or even how to dream." Goals are where the "rubber meets the road" or where we need to be accountable for taking action to make our dreams a reality.

Getting into and going to college is only a goal, a step along the way toward realizing your dreams. One of the defining characteristics of a goal is that it is a statement about what you will do or accomplish and by when—for example, "My goal is to earn acceptance to Tufts University by May of this year." Notice the "what" (earning acceptance into Tufts University) and the "when" (by May). Other examples of goal statements would be: "I score 100 points higher on my GRE's" and "I tell two teachers/people who will be my recommenders my dreams for my life so that they can get to know me better and include these sentiments in their letters."

Goals bridge your higher purpose, dreams, and commitments, to the strategies that you will use to manifest these. Include information about all of your future goals: school, grades, GRE scores, theatrical performances, social life, family relationships, physical conditioning, mental well-being, and accomplishments, among others.

Your goals should excite you, empower you to act, and be congruent with your dreams; meaning they should be things you want to accomplish. President Franklin D. Roosevelt prepared a long list of goals for his life when he was 14 years old, and on this list was becoming President of the United States!

Helpful Hint: Here are some characteristics of an effective goal statement:

1. Present tense (e.g. "I will finish my college essay for Tufts on or before September 7.")
2. Includes specific references to your broader visions or dreams for your life
3. Includes information about all of your future goals: school, family, relationships, work, spiritual, social, physical, emotional, financial, others
4. Congruent with your values and life purpose, and life dreams
5. Are precise and concise; about one or two sentences in length

My Goals are:

The "How" Contextual Levels of Understanding

Strategies, Plans, and Tactics

Getting into and going to college is a goal, a step along the way toward realizing your dreams. Then, by example, you need to formulate strategies, plans, and tactics that will help you achieve this goal. Usually we consider many strategic alternatives for each of our goals, and decide among them and then pursue. As an example, you may be following two strategies (and corresponding plans and tactics for your college acceptances)—the first strategy may be to apply to Tufts University and the second strategy to apply to other universities. In other words, you will achieve your goal of college acceptance into the best college match for you and your dreams and life purpose, whether it be through Tufts or another equally good college match.

Completing the Success Predictor is an integral part of these strategies, and you are taking action steps, or tactics, that fulfill the plan. Strategies, plans, and tactics therefore answer the question "how" to achieve goals and visions.

By way of another example, if you want to travel to Chicago over the summer to visit Northwestern University, then two possible plan you could follow could be (1) drive taking Route 80 through Pennsylvania, or (2) take an airplane. Both would lead to achieving the plan of travel to Chicago.

In this category you will formulate concrete plans and action steps or tactics for each strategic alternative. You could also plan on visiting friends or family if you choose to drive to Chicago, or visit other colleges in the Chicago area if you choose to fly. Then, if you like the plan to visit friends and family, then make your request for a good meal upon your arrival!

Helpful Hint: Here are some characteristics of effective strategies and plans:

1. Tied directly to specific goals (e.g. "I will apply to Tufts and to other potential colleges.")
2. Include specific references to your goals for your life.
3. Include information about all of your future goals: school, family, relationships, work, spiritual, social, physical, emotional, financial, others
4. Congruent with your values and life purpose, and life dreams
5. List each of your goals formulated in the previous section/category, and then formulate one or two strategic alternatives for each.
6. Plans and tactics should be tied directly to each strategic alternative and be very specific in their descriptions.

My Strategies, Plans, and Tactics for each of my goals are:

The "Evidence" Contextual Level of Understanding

Results

Results provide evidence that you are on the right track toward manifesting your purpose, vision, goals, and plans. Results serve as a compass; they are what occurs after you take action.

Results are what you have in your life, and you can check in with yourself to determine if the results you have produced are what you want in your life and whether they align with your dreams and goals.

Results can be intangible, such as feelings of excitement and pride upon acceptance into college, and tangible, such as the actual college acceptance letters.

You are producing results constantly in your life whether tangible or intangible, and you can determine if these are the ones you want, that represent your higher purpose and mission in life, or not.

Sometimes it is helpful to begin with the results in mind as a focus, and then determine the other categories from this level of understanding. Ask what results you want to produce in your life and in the world, and then work your way back up the Success Predictor categories.

These results you want to produce should be closely aligned with those you formulated in your vision statement.

The Results I want to produce are:

The Success Predictor Contextual Paradigm in Correct Order or Hierarchy

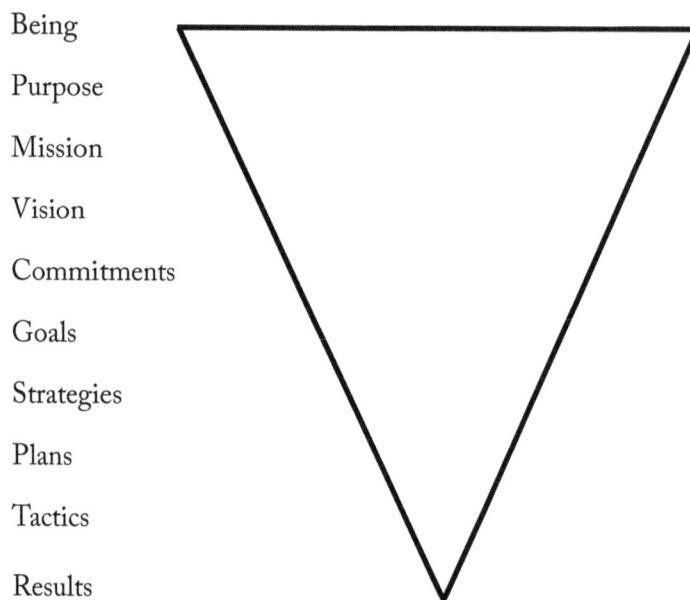

Being

Purpose

Mission

Vision

Commitments

Goals

Strategies

Plans

Tactics

Results

Recommendations for Teachers

Teachers can strengthen their students' self-knowledge and well-being in both simple and complex ways. Teachers can:

- Encourage students to complete the Success Predictor and discuss it with them.
- Read the iSelf distinctions and incorporate at least one distinction into an assignment, noting for students when they have strengthened their awareness of the distinction. For example, self-efficacy can be demonstrated by defending a mathematical theorem, and locus of control can be demonstrated by designing a recycling program in the school district.
- Explore ways to incorporate emotional learning in cognitive assignments, such as connecting assignments to making a meaningful contribution to the community.
- Form a departmental group to explore ways to encourage and recognize students' self-knowledge and self-responsibility.
- Engage colleagues in discussing ways to improve policies for integration of Self Across the Curriculum.

Teachers and school counselors can make a significant difference by developing programs for students, working with each other across departments, and reaching up through the hierarchies of leadership for school-wide change. Front-line educators can:

- Hold intra- and interdepartmental discussions on the best practices in this *Toolkit* to explore ones to incorporate into their functions and schools.
- Develop preventative programming based on the iSelf model's self-system and positive psychology attributions.
- Create new student handbooks and other resources.
- Build the Success Predictor into home-room programs.
- Develop four-year programs that support students' progress towards their personal, college, and professional goals.
- Design metrics to measure students' well-being.
- Train faculty in the many ways to impart well-being and self-knowledge using the *Mental Health for All Toolkit*.
- Make presentations to school leaders and community members on the iSelf distinctions they feel are most important to include in the school's mission and in interdepartmental programs.

Teachers can reach across grade levels and administrative functions to initiate school-wide systems of support for mental health and wellness. Schools should bring together representatives from mental health, counseling, and teaching functions and other leaders to:

- Develop a new mission statement that puts well-being at the center of the school.
- Develop a school-wide plan for tangible and integrated programs that deliver on the promise of the well-being mission.
- Determine school-wide themes to engage students in making a difference in society.
- Design metrics to measure how the new well-being mission is helping to achieve school-wide goals.
- Work with information technology professionals to develop online systems for students to self-manage their goals, competencies, and accomplishments.
- Redesign education programs to include the values of well-being, self-knowledge, and societal contribution.

Recommendations for Parents

Parents can help their children by discussing the purpose and dreams that their children prepared as a Success Predictor exercise, in order to reinforce the depth of meaning. Additionally, through everyday observations, when a child exhibits achieving a portion of the dream/vision, acknowledge and celebrate it.

Recommendations for Students

Students can:

- Complete the Success Predictor to proactively develop a structure to accomplish their goals and pursue their dreams in college and in life.
- Read and learn more about the iSelf distinctions, and provide themselves with a new awareness of the self-system and positive psychology attributions that have been shown to lead to positive life trajectories.
- Develop peer-to-peer counseling groups to discuss the iSelf distinctions, complete the Success Predictor, and encourage self-authorship.
- Reach out to faculty and student success professionals to engage in extracurricular and community-based projects.
- Create groups to meet with school leaders and discuss needs and request resources to support their well-being.
- Continue to voice that the purpose of education is well-being for self, family, friends, institutions, and society.

Example for Students: Aligning Life Purpose and Career Using the Success Predictor

The Success Predictor assessment instrument was administered in a short workshop format to high school students. The Center for the Self in Schools offered a short, one-day, three session workshop to help students understand their life purpose and dreams, then choose their academic program based upon those dreams, and then select a potential career path and internships that would manifest such expressions of themselves.

The result? Students took it upon themselves to take ownership of their well-being and future directions.

For example, one student who had limited financial means to even attend college expressed an interest in pursuing a "practical" career after high school to satisfy her parents' demands. As such, she was just going through the motions of attending classes and was not emotionally engaged in her high school courses. Through the workshop, she transformed her understanding of who she was and what she was meant to do with her life—the distinct difference she could make.

She changed her academic focus from Spanish to International Relations, and she then actively found and accepted a summer internship in Peru. She went on to attend a prestigious college, after which she worked to empower inner-city people to make their communities and neighborhoods safer and cleaner and to improve their personal health by reducing obesity rates. Her self-esteem and confidence soared, giving rise to a dynamic personality that had lain dormant.

Final Thoughts—
Mental Health for All and the Future

As trustees of the human condition and providers of the pathway to the good life, let us search for new ways to realize our highest visions for what is possible. We believe that it is indeed possible to do more and to help people take action to create a better society.

We can teach people how not to hate others who are different than ourselves. We can teach empathy, taking new perspectives on how to have a view of self and life that is inclusive and actually cares for others because of their differences, not in spite of them. We can teach how to handle the emotion of anger, with strategies to express it appropriately and more effectively. We can teach people a mind-set that allows for uncertainty, complexity, and how to process change effectively. We can take care of people preventatively, rather than reacting to crises. We can teach people how to connect with their innate goodness and contribute to a better society and life for all. We can make well-being our mission.

Poor self-knowledge is associated with a broad range of mental disorders and social problems, including depression, suicidal tendencies, eating disorders, and anxiety, substance abuse, violence, and identity disorders. Self-knowledge is the number one protective factor for mental health. We can help teachers and school counselors focus on teaching self-knowledge as the key to academic and career success and also as a mental illness prevention model. We can help teachers, parents, and counselors focus on teaching self-knowledge and well-being; then people who are mentally ill will be noticed and helped far earlier, and those at risk will have many more healthy pathways to health and well-being.

Schools and families often seem to add to the anxiety in our society by overemphasizing power, external accomplishments, and cognitive pursuits to the detriment of the whole person. We realize it represents a big paradigm shift to put self-knowledge and well-being at the top of a school's priorities, but it is the only way to reverse the tragic trends and loss of well-being in our country.

Our system of education actually shapes society; provide the leaders for our health care, business, and governmental organizations; and future leaders of our system of education. Therefore, educators, parents, and those in leadership positions have a moral responsibility to do everything they can to strengthen people's well-being.

Education can encourage humanity's deep hunger for expressing contributions to the greater good and the well-being of all. We have evolved as a human species, where know our consciousness is ready to create and witness acts of kindness and love.

We ourselves struggled with purpose and self-knowledge in our schooling years, although outwardly we were doing fine, and we searched for help from our institutions but did not know enough to ask, or felt stifled talking about human emotions and noncognitive needs in places that appeared to worship academic and intellectual cognition. So we took responsibility in our adult lives to help others who might be in a similar situation.

We believe, and deep inside ourselves know, that we can help by bringing all of the positive developments and knowledge about well-being into the mainstream of the education mission. What keeps us motivated is the possibility of actually impacting the human condition, of providing perspectives and approaches that can help people get on track and create pathways to happy, healthy, and flourishing lives. We are blessed to have discovered this for ourselves, and we hope to help others with what we have learned.

If you have been helped in some small way, either personally or professionally, by using this *Toolkit* as a teacher, parent, student, or in your life, you have honored us.

References and Resources

Achor, S. 2010. *The Happiness Advantage*. New York: Random House.

American Academy of Child and Adolescent Psychiatry. 2011. "Bullying." *Facts for Families*, March 2011. Accessed October 1, 2012. http://www.aacap.org/galleries/FactsForFamilies/80_bullying.pdf.

American College Personnel Association. 2008. *Professional Competencies: A Report of the Steering Committee on Professional Competencies.* http://www.myacpa.org/au/governance/docs/ACPA_Competencies.pdf

American College Personnel Association & National Association of Student Personnel Administrators. 2010. *ACPA/NASPA Professional Competency Areas for Student Affairs Practitioners.* Washington, DC: Authors. http://www.myacpa.org/professional-competency-areas-student-affairs-practitioners

American Federation of Teachers of New Jersey. 2012. "AFT Resolutions: Digital Learning in Pre-K–12 Instruction." Accessed October 1, 2012. http://www.aft.org/about/resolution_detail.cfm?articleid=1619.

American Psychiatric Association. 2000. *Diagnostic and Statistical Manual of Mental Disorders* (4th ed.). Arlington, VA: Author.

American Psychiatric Association. 2013. *Diagnostic and Statistical Manual of Mental Disorders* (5th ed.). Washington, DC: Author.

American Psychological Association Board of Educational Affairs. 1997. *Learner-Centered Psychological Principles: Framework for School Reform and Redesign.* Washington, DC: Center for Psychology in Schools and Education.

Anderson, J., Greeno, J., Reder, L., & Simon, H. A. 2000. "Perspectives on Learning, Thinking, and Activity." *Educational Researcher* 229(4): 11–13.

Anderson, J. R. 1995. *Learning and Memory*. New York: John Wiley & Sons.

Anderson, J. R., & Lebiere, C. 1998. *The Atomic Components of Thought*. Mahwah, NJ: Lawrence Erlbaum.

Annie E. Casey Foundation. 2012. "Kids Count Data Bank." Accessed October 1, 2012. http://www.aecf.org/MajorInitiatives/KIDSCOUNT.aspx.

Association of American Colleges and Universities. 2002. *Greater Expectations: A New Vision for Learning as the Nation Goes to College.* https://www.aacu.org/sites/default/files/files/publications/GreaterExpectations.pdf

Association of American Universities. 2015. *Report on the AAU Campus Climate Survey on Sexual Assault and Sexual Misconduct.* http://www.aau.edu/Climate-Survey.aspx?id=16525

Atkinson, R. C., & Shiffrin, R. M. 1968. "Human Memory: A Proposed System and Its Control Processes." In *The Psychology of Learning and Motivation* (Vol. 2), edited by K. Spence & J. Spence, pp. 89–195. New York: Academic Press.

Baker. D. P. 2009. *The Quiet Revolution: The Educational Transform of Modern Society* (Draft book manuscript, Pennsylvania State University). Draft copy available from dpb4@psu.edu.

Baker, D. P. 2014. *The Schooled Society: The Educational Transformation of Global Culture*. Stanford: Stanford University Press.

Baker, D. P., & LeTendre, J. 2005. *National Differences, Global Similarities: World Culture and the Future of Schooling*. Stanford, CA: Stanford University Press.

Baker Miller, J. 1976. *Toward a New Psychology of Women*. Boston: Beacon Press.

Bandura, A. 1986. *Social Foundations of Thought and Action: A Social Cognitive Theory*. Englewood Cliffs, NJ: Prentice-Hall.

Bandura, A. 1997. *Self-Efficacy: The Exercise of Control*. New York: Freeman.

Bandura, A., Barbaranelli, C., Caprara, G. V., & Pastorelli, C. 2001. "Self-Efficacy Beliefs as Shapers of Children's Aspirations and Career Trajectories." *Child Development* 72(1): 187–206.

Baumgardner, Ann H. 1990. "To Know Oneself Is to Like Oneself: Self-Certainty and Self-Affect." *Journal of Personality and Social Psychology* 58(6; June 1990): 1062–72.

Berger, K. S., & Thompson, R. A. 1995. *The Developing Person Through Childhood and Adolescence*. New York: Worth.

Berger, P. L., and Luckmann, T. 1966. *The Social Construction of Reality*. New York: Random House.

Bernanke, B. S. 2012. "Economic Measurement." Paper presented at the 32nd General Conference of the International Association for Research in Income and Wealth, Cambridge, MA, August 6. Accessed October 1, 2012. http://www.federalreserve.gov/newsevents/speech/bernanke20120806a.htm.

Blackburn, I. M., Eunson, K. M., & Bishop, S. 1986. "A Two-Year Naturalistic Follow-Up of Depressed Patients Treated With Cognitive Therapy, Pharmacotherapy and a Combination of Both." *Journal of Affective Disorders* 10: 67–75.

Blume, G. W., & Heckman, D. S. 1997. "What Do Students Know About Algebra and Functions?" In *Results From the Sixth Mathematics Assessment*, edited by P. A. Kenney & E. A. Silver, pp. 225–77. Reston, VA: National Council of Teachers of Mathematics.

Borysenko, J. 1987. *Minding the Body, Mending the Mind*. Reading, MA: Addison-Wesley.

Borysenko, J. 1994. *A Women's Journey to God: Finding the Feminine Path*. New York: Riverhead Books.

Bostock, D. 1986. *Plato's Phaedo*. Oxford: Clarendon Press.

Bouffard-Bouchard, T. 1990. Influence of Self-Efficacy on Performance in a Cognitive Task. *Journal of Social Psychology* 130, 353–63.

Bourdieu, P. 1977. "Cultural Reproduction and Social Reproduction." In *Power and Ideology in Education*, edited by J. Karabel & A. H. Halsey, pp. 487–511. New York: Oxford University Press.

Bourdieu, P. 1986. "The Forms of Capital." In *Handbook of Theory and Research for the Sociology of Education*, edited by J. G. Richardson, pp. 241–58. New York: Greenwood Press.

Bradie, M., & Harms, W. 2012. "Evolutionary Epistemology." In *The Stanford Encyclopedia of Philosophy* (Spring 2012 ed.), edited by E. N. Zalta. Stanford, CA: Stanford University Press.

Branden, N. 1994. *The Six Pillars of Self-Esteem*. New York: Bantam Books.

Broadie, S. 2001. "Soul and Body in Plato and Decartes." *Proceedings of the Aristotelian Society* 101: 295–308.

Brown, F., & LaJambe, C. 2016. *Positive Psychology and Well Being: Applications for Enhanced Living.* San Diego, CA: Cognella.

Bruner, J. 1960. *The Process of Education.* Cambridge, MA: Harvard University Press.

Bruner, J. 1996. *The Culture of Education.* Cambridge, MA: Harvard University Press.

Brzycki, E. J. and Brzycki, H. G. 2016. *Student Success in Higher Education: Developing the Whole Person through High-Impact Practices.* State College, PA: BG Publishing.

Brzycki, H. G. 2009. "Teacher Beliefs and Classroom Practices That Impart Self-System and Positive Psychology Attributes." PhD diss., Penn State University. https://etda.libraries.psu.edu/paper/9451/5058.

Brzycki, H. G. 2010. "The Self in Teaching and Learning." In *Educational Psychology Reader: The Art and Science of How People Learn*, edited by G. S. Goodman. New York: Peter Lang.

Brzycki, H. G. 2013. *The Self in Schooling: Theory and Practice: How to Create Happy, Healthy and Flourishing Children in the 21 Century.* State College, PA: BG Publishing.

Bullying Statistics. 2009. "Bullying Statistics—Stop Bullying, Harassment, and Violence." Accessed October 1, 2012. http://www.bullyingstatistics.org.

Butler County Community College. 2016. *Promoting Student Success and Retention at BC3.* http://www.bc3.edu/services/pdf/oral-presentations.pdf

California State University. 2016. *Academic and Student Success Programs: High Impact Practices Systematically.* Conference at Hotel Fullerton Anaheim. https://www.calstate.edu/engage/conference/documents/2016-ASSP-Conference-program.pdf

Caplan, M. 2009. *Eyes Wide Open: Cultivating Discernment on the Spiritual Path.* Boulder, CO: Sounds True.

Card, S., Moran, T., & Newell, A. 1983. *The Psychology of Human-Computer Interaction.* Hillsdale, NJ: Lawrence Erlbaum.

Carlstrom, A. (Ed.). 2013. *NACADA National Survey of Academic Advising* (Monograph No. 25). Manhattan, KS: National Academic Advising Association. http://www.nacada.ksu.edu/Resources/Clearinghouse/View-Articles/Advisor-Load.aspx

Center for Collegiate Mental Health. (2016, January). *2015 Annual Report* (Publication No. STA 15-108) http://ccmh.psu.edu/wpcontent/uploads/sites/3058/2016/01/2015_CCMH_Report_1-18-2015.pdf

Center for Community College Engagement. 2015. "Community College Survey of Student Engagement." The University of Texas at Austin. http://www.ccsse.org/survey/survey.cfm

Center for Community College Student Engagement. 2012. *A Matter of Degrees: Promising Practices for Community College Student Success (A First Look).* Austin, TX: The University of Texas at Austin, Community College Leadership Program.

Centers for Disease Control and Prevention. 1999. "Improving Child and Adolescent Health Through Physical Activity and Nutrition." Accessed October 1, 2012. http://www.cdc.gov/nccdphp/dnpa/panprog.htm.

Centers for Disease Control and Prevention. 2005. "CDC Efforts to Reduce or Prevent Obesity." Accessed October 1, 2012. http://www.cdc.gov/OD/OC/MEDIA/pressrel/fs050419.htm.

Centers for Disease Control and Prevention. 2007. "Teen Suicide Rate: Highest Increase in 15 Years." Accessed October 1, 2012. http://www.sciencedaily.com/releases/2007/09/070907221530.htm.

Centers for Disease Control and Prevention. 2010. "Current Depression Among Adults—United States, 2006 and 2008." *MMWR* 59(38): 1229–1235.

Centers for Disease Control and Prevention. 2011. "Antidepressant Use in Persons Aged 12 and Over: United States, 2005–2008." *National Center for Health Statistics Brief*, no. 76. Accessed October 1, 2012. http://www.cdc.gov/nchs/data/databriefs/db76.htm.

Centers for Disease Control and Prevention. 2012a. "Adult Obesity Facts." Accessed October 1, 2012. http://www.cdc.gov/obesity/data/adult.html.

Centers for Disease Control and Prevention. 2012b. "National Vital Statistics System—Mortality." http://www.cdc.gov/nchs/deaths.htm

Child Trends Data Bank. 2012. "Adolescents Who Felt Sad or Hopeless: Indicators on Children and Youth." http://www.childtrendsdatabank.org/sites/default/files/30_Felt_Sad_or_Hopeless.pdf.

Chingos, M., & Whitehurst, G. 2012. *Choosing Blindly: Instructional Materials, Teacher Effectiveness, and the Common Core*. Washington, DC: The Brookings Institution.

Christianson, S. A, ed. 1992. *The Handbook of Emotion and Memory*. Hillsdale, NJ: Lawrence Erlbaum.

Clemson University. 2012. "Olweus Bullying Prevention Program." Accessed October 1, 2012. http://www.clemson.edu/olweus.

Cohen, E. 2007. "CDC: Antidepressants Most Prescribed Drug in U.S." Accessed October 1, 2012. http://articles.cnn.com/2007–07–09/health/antidepressants_1_antidepressants-high-blood-pressure-drugs-psychotropic-drugs?_s=PM:HEALTH.

Cohen, J. 2006. "Social, Emotional, Ethical, and Academic Education: Creating a Climate for Learning, Participation in Democracy, and Well-Being." *Harvard Educational Review* 76: 2.

Cohen, S., Doyle, W. J., Treanor, J. J., & Turner, R. B. 2006. "Positive Emotional Style Predicts Resistance to Illness After Experimental Exposure to Rhinovirus or Influenza A Virus." *Journal of Bio-Behavioral Medicine* 68(6): 809–815.

Cohen, S., Doyle, W. J., Turner, R. B., Alper, C. M., & Skoner, D. P. 2006. "Research Highlight: Emotional Style and Susceptibility to the Common Cold." In *Healthier Lives Through Behavioral and Social Science Research*. Available from the Office of Behavioral and Social Sciences Research website: http://obssr.od.nih.gov/publications/books_and_projects/books_and_reports.aspx.

Cole, M. 1996. *Cultural Psychology*. Cambridge, MA: Harvard University Press.

Coleman, J. 1988. "Social Capital in the Creation of Human Capital." *American Journal of Sociology* 94(Suppl.): S95–S120.

Coles, R. 1997a. "Basic Humanity." (Transcript of interview with David Gergen.) *MacNeil/Lehrer News Hour*. Accessed October 1, 2012. http://www.pbs.org/newshour/gergen/february97/coles_2–21.html.

Coles, R. 1997b. *The Moral Intelligence of Children*. New York: Random House.

Collins, J. L. 1982. "Self-Efficacy and Ability in Achievement Behavior." Paper presented at the Annual Meeting of the American Educational Research Association, New York, March.

Copernicus, N., & Duncan, A. M., trans. 1976. *On the Revolutions of the Heavenly Spheres*. New York: Barnes and Noble.

Cornell University. 2014. "University Launches 'Engaged Cornell' with $50 million Gift." *Cornell Chronicle*. http://news.cornell.edu/stories/2014/10/university-launches-engaged-cornell-50-million-gift

Cornell University. 2015. "Cornell University at Its Sesquicentennial: A Strategic Plan 2010-2015." https://www.cornell.edu/strategicplan/docs/060410-strategic-plan-summary.pdf

Cornell University. 2016. "Gannett Health Center: Building Resilience." https://www.gannett.cornell.edu/topics/resilience/index.cfm

Corno, L., & Mandinach, E. B. 1983. "The Role of Cognitive Engagement in Classroom Learning and Motivation." *Educational Psychologist* 18: 88–108.

Council of Chief State School Officers. 2006. E-Newsletter, Spring, p. 5. Washington, DC: CCSSO.

Couture, R. 2016. *Impactful Advising: Investing in Students' Lives*. Manuscript submitted for publication.

Cremin, L. A. 1964. *The Transformation of the School: Progressivism in American Education 1876–1957*. New York: Vintage/Random House.

Cresta, B. 2004. "The National Context." Paper presented at Managed Behavioral Health Care in Massachusetts: Challenges of Maintaining Access and Quality. Schneider Institute for Health Policy. Accessed October 1, 2012. http://www.sihp.brandeis.edu/shedard/downloads.html.

Crook, T. R., Todd, S. Y., Combs, J. G., Woehr, D. J., & Ketchen, D. J. 2011. "Does Human Capital Matter? A Meta-Analysis of the Relationship Between Human Capital and Firm Performance." *Journal of Applied Psychology* 96(3): 443–456.

Csikszentmihalyi, M. 1993. *The Evolving Self*. New York: HarperCollins.

Csikszentmihalyi, M. 1997. *Creativity: Flow and the Psychology of Discovery and Invention*. New York: HarperCollins.

Curtin, S. C., Warner, M., & Hedegaard, H. 2016. *Increase in Suicide in the United States, 1999–2014*. NCHS data brief no. 241. Hyattsville, MD: National Center for Health Statistics.

Cuseo, J. 2008. "Assessing Advisor Effectiveness." In *Academic Advising: A Comprehensive Handbook* (2nd ed.), edited by V. N. Gordon, W. R. Habley, & T. J. Grites, pp. 369–385. San Francisco: Jossey-Bass.

Damasio, A. 1994. *Descartes' Error: Emotion, Reason, and the Human Brain*. New York: Penguin.

Davis, J. V. 2003. "Transpersonal Psychology." In *The Encyclopedia of Religion and Nature*, edited by B. Taylor & J. Kaplan. Bristol, England: Thoemmes Continuum.

Deci, E. L., & Ryan, R. M. 1985. *Intrinsic Motivation and Self-Determination in Human Behavior*. New York: Cambridge University Press.

Deci, E. L., & Ryan, R. M. 1995. "Human Autonomy: The Basis for True Self-Esteem." In *Efficacy, Agency, and Self-Esteem*, edited by M. Kernis, pp. 31–49. New York: Plenum.

Deci, E. L., & Ryan, R. M. 2008. "Facilitating Optimal Motivation and Psychological Well-Being Across Life's Domains." *Canadian Psychology* 49: 14–23.

Deci, E. L., Nezlek, J., & Sheinman, L. 1981. "Characteristics of the Rewarder and Intrinsic Motivation of the Rewardee." *Journal of Personality and Social Psychology* 40: 1–10.

Deming, W. E. 1986. *Out of the Crisis*. Boston: MIT Press.

Dewey, J. 1900. *The School and Society*. Chicago: University of Chicago Press.

Dewey, J. 1902. *The Child and the Curriculum*. Chicago: University of Chicago Press.

Dewey, J. 1916. *Democracy and Education*. New York: Macmillan.

Diener, E., Lucas, R. E., & Oishi, S. 2002. "Subjective Well-Being: The Science of Happiness and Life Satisfaction." In *The Handbook of Positive Psychology*, edited by C. R. Snyder & S. J. Lopez, pp. 463–473. New York: Oxford University Press.

DiMaggio, P. 1997. "Culture and Cognition." *Annual Review of Sociology* 23: 263–287.

DiMaggio, P. 1997. "Culture and Cognition." *Annual Review of Sociology* 23: 263–87.

Dokoupil, T. 2012. "Is the Onslaught Making Us Crazy?" *Newsweek*, July 16.

Dolcos, F., LaBar, K., & Cabeza, R. 2004. "Interaction Between the Amygdala and the Medial Temporal Lobe Memory System Predicts Better Memory for Emotional Events." *Neuron* 42: 855–863.

Dolcos, F., & McCarthy, G. 2006. "Brain Systems Mediating Cognitive Interference by Emotional Distraction." *Journal of Neuroscience* 26(7): 2072–2079.

Dowell, D., Haegerich, T. M., & Chou, R. 2016. "CDC Guideline for Prescribing Opioids for Chronic Pain—United States." *MMWR Recomm Rep* 65: 1–49.

Duckworth, A. L., Steen, T. A., & Seligman, M. E. P. 2005. "Positive Psychology in Clinical Practice." *Annual Review of Clinical Psychology* 1: 629–651.

Durham, T. 2015. *University of Kansas, Student Affairs Impact Report, 2014–2015*. https://studentaffairs.ku.edu/sites/studentaffairs.ku.edu/files/docs/SA_Impact_Report%20Final_2015.pdf

Eagan, K., Stolzenberg, E. B., Ramirez, J. J., Aragon, M. C., Suchard, M. R., & Hurtado, S. 2014. *The American Freshman: National Norms, Fall 2014*. Los Angeles: Higher Education Research Institute, UCLA. http://www.heri.ucla.edu

Edformation. 2004. *AIMSweb Training DVD: Illustrations and Practice Exercises for Use With AIMSweb Administration and Scoring Guides* (Video). Eden Prairie, MN: Edformation.

Edwards, V. J., Anda, R. F., Dube, S. R., Dong, M., Chapman, D. F., & Felitti, V. J. 2005. "The Wide-Ranging Health Consequences of Adverse Childhood Experiences." In *Victimization of Children and Youth: Patterns of Abuse, Response Strategies*, edited by K. Kendall-Tackett & S. Giacomoni. Kingston, NJ: Civic Research Institute.

Effrat, A. 1972. "Power to the Paradigms." *Sociological Inquiry* 42(3–4): 3–33.

Elliot, A. J., & McGregor, H. A. 2001. "A 2 by 2 Achievement Goal Framework." *Journal of Personality and Social Psychology* 80(3): 501–519.

EPE Research Center. 2008. "Graduation Rates in America's Top 50 Cities." Accessed October 1, 2012. http://www.edweek.org/info/about/research.html.

Erikson, E. 1963. *Childhood and Society*. New York: Norton.

Erikson, E. 1968. *Identity, Youth, and Crisis*. New York: Norton.

Erikson, E. 1980. *Identity and the Life Cycle*. New York: Norton.

Falce, L. May 2016. "Penn State Sees Increase in Self-Injury Cases, Suicidal Ideation." *Centre Daily Times*. http://www.centredaily.com/news/local/education/penn-state/article75776342.html#storylink=cpy

Farrington, C. A. April 2013. *Academic Mind-sets as a Critical Component of Deeper Learning*. White paper prepared for the William and Flora Hewlett Foundation.

Felitti, V. J., & Anda, R. F., 2009. "The Relationship of Adverse Childhood Experiences to Adult Medical Disease, Psychiatric Disorders, and Sexual Behavior: Implications for Healthcare." In *The Hidden Epidemic: The Impact of Early Life Trauma on Health and Disease*, edited by R. Lanius & E. Vermetten. Cambridge: Cambridge University Press. http://www.unnaturalcauses.org/assets/uploads/file/ACE%20Study-Lanius.pdf

Felitti, V. J., Anda, R. F., Nordenberg, D., Williamson, D. F., Spitz, A. M., Edwards, V., Koss, M. P., & Marks, J. S. 1998. "Relationship of Childhood Abuse and Household Dysfunction to Many of the Leading Causes of Death in Adults: The Adverse Childhood Experiences (ACE) Study." *American Journal of Preventive Medicine* 14: 245–258.

Festinger, L. 1957. *A Theory of Cognitive Dissonance*. Stanford: Stanford University Press.

Feuer, M., & Towne, L. 2002. "The Logic and the Basic Principles of Scientific-Based Research." Accessed October 1, 2012. http://www.ed.gov/nclb/methods/whatworks/research/page_pg11.html.

Finkelstein, E. A., Fiebelkorn, I. C., & Wang, G. 2003. "National Medical Spending Attributable to Overweight and Obesity: How Much, and Who's Paying?" *Health Affairs* W3: 219–226.

Florida State University. 2016. *The Center for Academic Retention and Enhancement* (CARE). http://care.fsu.edu/College-Programs/CARE-College-Life-Coaching

Fox, M. 2008. *Reading Magic: Why Reading Aloud to Our Children Will Change Their Lives Forever*. Orlando, FL: Harvest Original-Harcourt.

Frankl, V. 1984. *Man's Search for Meaning*. New York: Simon & Schuster.

Freire, P. 2000. *Pedagogy of the Oppressed*. New York: Continuum.

Gardner, H. 1983. *Frames of Mind: The Theory of Multiple Intelligences*. New York: Basic Books.

Gardner, H. 2000. *The Disciplined Mind*. New York: Penguin.

Gersten, R., Baker, S., & Lloyd, J. W. 2000. "Designing High-Quality Research in Special Education: Group Experimental Design." *Journal of Special Education* 34(1): 2–18.

Giffin, W. M. 1906. *School Days in the Fifties*. Chicago: A. Flanagan Company.

Glas, G. 2006. "Person, Personality, Self, and Identity: A Philosophically Informed Conceptual Analysis." *Journal of Personality Disorders* 20: 126–138.

Glasersfeld, E. von. 1995. *Radical Constructivism: A Way of Knowing and Learning*. London: Falmer Press.

Glennen, R. E. 1975. "Intrusive College Counseling." *College Student Journal* 9(1). http://www.nacada.ksu.edu/Resources/Academic-Advising-Today/View-Articles/Proactive-(Intrusive)-Advising!.aspx#sthash.ZLRKeRko.dpuf

Goetz, T., Zirngibl, A., Pekrun, R., & Hall, N. 2003. "Emotions, Learning and Achievement From an Educational-Psychological Perspective." In *Learning Emotions: The Influence of Affective Factors on Classroom Learning*, edited by P. Mayring & C. von Rhoeneck, pp. 9–28. Frankfurt, Germany: Peter Lang.

Goldberg, M., & Cross, C. 2005. "Time Out: Rethinking the Hours America Spends Educating." Accessed October 1, 2012. http://www.edutopia.org/time-out-rethinking-hours-america-educates.

Goleman, D. 1995. *Emotional Intelligence: Why It Can Matter More Than IQ*. New York: Bantam Books.

Goodman, E., & Whitaker, R. C. 2002. "A Prospective Study on the Role of Depression in the Development and Persistence of Obesity." *Pediatrics* 110(3): 497–504.

Goodman, G., ed. 2010. *Educational Psychology Reader: The Art and Science of How People Learn*. New York: Peter Lang.

Greenberg, P. E., Stiglin, L. E., Finkelstein, S. N., & Berndt, E. R. 1993. "The Economic Burden of Depression in 1990." *Journal of Clinical Psychiatry* 54: 405–426.

Greene, M. 1995. *Releasing the Imagination*. San Francisco: Jossey-Bass.

Greer, R. D. 2002. "Designing Teaching Strategies: An Applied Behavior Analysis Systems Approach." In *Educational Psychology Series: Critical Reviews of Research Knowledge, Theories, Principles, and Practices*, edited by G. Phye. New York: Academic Press.

Greeson, J. 1993. *It's Not What You Are Eating; It's What Eating You: The 28-Day Plan to Heal Hidden Food Addiction*. New York: Simon & Schuster.

Grites, T. J. 2013. "Developmental Academic Advising: A 40-Year Context." *NACADA Journal* 33(1): 5–15. http://www.nacada.ksu.edu/Resources/Journal/Download-Journal-Articles.aspx

Hanushek, E. A., Peterson, P. E., & Woessmann, L. 2012. *Achievement Growth: International and U.S. States Trends in Student Performance*. PEPG report no. 12–13. http://hks.harvard.edu/pepg.

Harter, S. 1999. *The Construction of the Self: A Developmental Perspective*. New York: Guilford Press.

Harter, S., & Marold, D. 1992. "Psychosocial Risk Factors Contributing to Adolescent Suicidal Ideation." In *Child and Adolescent Suicide: Clinical Developmental Perspectives*, edited by G. Noam & S. Borst. Rochester, NY: University of Rochester Press.

Harvey, O. J. 1986. "Belief Systems and Attitudes Toward the Death Penalty and Other Punishments." *Journal of Personality* 54: 659–675.

Hawkins, D. J., Kosterman, R., Catalano, R. F., Hill, K. G., & Abbott, R. D. 2008. "Effects of Social Development Intervention in Childhood 15 Years Later." *Archives of Pediatric and Adolescent Medicine* 162(12): 1133–1141.

Heckhausen, H. 1977. "Achievement Motivation and Its Constructs: A Cognitive Model." *Motivation and Emotion* 1(4): 283–329.

Heckhausen, H., ed. 2000. *Motivational Psychology of Human Development*. Oxford: Elsevier.

Henderson, J., & Hawthorne, R. 2000. *Transformative Curriculum Leadership*. Upper Saddle River, NJ: Pearson Education.

Henriques, G. 2014. "The College Student Mental Health Crisis." *Psychology Today*. https://www.psychologytoday.com/blog/theory-knowledge/201402/the-college-student-mental-health-crisis

Hensley, S. 2011. "Look Around: 1 in 10 Adults Takes Antidepressants." SHOTS: NPR Health Blog, October 10. http://www.npr.org/blogs/health/2011/10/20/141544135/look-around-1-in-10-americans-take-antidepressants.

Herman, K. C., Lambert, S. F., Reinke, W. M., & Ialongo, N. S. 2008. "Low Academic Competence in First Grade as a Risk Factor for Depressive Cognitions and Symptoms in Middle School." *Journal of Counseling Psychology* 55(3): 400–410.

Hermes, J. J. 2008. "Report Shows Stunning Failures in High-School Graduation Rates." *Chronicle of Higher Education*. Accessed October 1, 2012. http://chronicle.com/article/Report-Shows-Stunning-Failures/40728.

Hiebert, J., & Carpenter, T. 1992. "Learning and Teaching With Understanding." In *Handbook of Research on Mathematics Teaching and Learning*, edited by D. Grouws, pp. 65–97. New York: Simon & Schuster Macmillan.

Hillman, J. 1996. *The Soul's Code: In Search of Character and Calling*. New York: Random House.

Hillman, J. 1999. *The Force of Character and the Lasting Life*. New York: Random House.

Hoelscher, D. M., Day, R. S., Lee, E. S., Frankowski, R. F., Kelder, S. H., Ward, J. L., & Scheurer, M. E. 2004. "Measuring the Prevalence of Overweight in Texas School Children." *American Journal of Public Health* 94: 1002–1008.

Hoffman, J. L., & Bresciani, M. J. (2012). "Identifying What Student Affairs Professionals Value: A Mixed Methods Analysis of Professional Competencies Listed in Job Descriptions." *Research and Practice in Assessment*, 7(1), 26–40. http://go.galegroup.com/ps/i.do?id=GALE%7CA339254319&v=2.1&u=ksu&it=r&p=AONE&sw=w&asid=3a8f2f636f2ee220a73aacafa511ac74

Home Box Office. 2012. *Weight of the Nation*. Accessed October 1, 2012. http://theweightofthenation.hbo.com/films/main-films.

Immordino-Yang, M. H. 2008. *The Relevance of Social and Affective Neuroscience to Education* (Video). Presented at USC Rossier School of Education Brown Bag Series. Accessed October 1, 2012. http://m.youtube.com/#/watch?v=KyjatC2MCYY.

Immordino-Yang, M. H., & Damasio, A. 2007. "We Feel, Therefore We Learn: The Relevance of Affective and Social Neuroscience to Education." *Mind, Brain, and Education* 1(1): 3–10.

Immordino-Yang, M. H., & Faeth, M. 2010. "The Role of Emotion and Skilled Intuition in Learning." In *Mind, Brain, and Education: Neuroscience Implications for the Classroom*, edited by D. Sousa. Bloomington, IN: Solution Tree/Leading Edge.

Immordino-Yang, M. H., & Fischer, K. W. 2009a. "Brain Development." In *Corsini Encyclopedia of Psychology* (4th ed.), edited by I. Weiner & E. Craighead. New York: John Wiley & Sons.

Immordino-Yang, M. H., & Fischer, K. W. 2009b. "Neuroscience Bases of Learning." In *International Encyclopedia of Education* (3rd ed.), edited by V. G. Aukrust. Oxford, England: Elsevier.

Indiana University Center for Postsecondary Research. 2015. *The Carnegie Classification of Institutions of Higher Education, 2015 edition*, Bloomington, IN: Author.

International Assessments of Counseling Services (IACS). 2014. *Standards for University and College Counseling Services*. Alexandria, VA: Author. http://0201.nccdn.net/1_2/000/000/0ce/fa4/IACS-STANDARDS-updated-9-24-2015.pdf

International Association of Counseling Services. 2014. *National Survey of College Counseling Centers*. Monograph Series Number 9V. http://www.collegecounseling.org/wp-content/uploads/NCCCS2014_v2.pdf

Izard, C. E. 1984. "Emotion-Cognition Relationships and Human Development." In *Emotions, Cognition, and Behavior*, edited by C. E. Izard, J. Kagan, & R. B. Zajonc. New York: Cambridge University Press.

Jahoda, M. 1958. *Current Concepts of Positive Mental Health*. New York: Basic Books.

Jalali, A. A., & Mahmoodi, H. 2009. "Virtual Age: Next Wave of Change in Society." Paper presented at the 2009 International Joint Conferences on e-CASE and e-Technology, Singapore, January 8–10.

James, W. 1890. *Principles of Psychology* (Vol. 1). New York: Henry Holt and Company.

James, W. 1892. *Psychology (Briefer Course)*. New York: The Library of America.

Johnson, M. H. 2001. "Functional Brain Development in Humans." *Nature Reviews: Neuroscience* 2(7): 475–483.

Jung, C. G. 1961. *Memories, Dreams, Reflections*, edited by Aniela Jaffé. New York: Vintage Books.

Kegan, J. 1994. *In Over Our Heads: The Mental Demands of Modern Life*. Cambridge, MA: Harvard University Press.

Keltner, D. 2009. *Born to Be Good*. New York: Norton.

Kensinger, E. A., & Corkin, S. 2004. "Two Routes to Emotional Memory: Distinct Neural Processes for Valence and Arousal." *Proceedings of the National Academy of Sciences USA* 101: 3310–3115.

Kittredge, C. 2004. "N. H. Explores Worldly Ways to Learn." *Boston Globe*, May 16.

Kroger, J. 1996. "Identity, Regression and Development." *Journal of Adolescence* 19: 203–222.

Kuh, G. D. 2008. *High-Impact Educational Practices: What They Are, Who Has Access to Them, and Why They Matter*. AAC&U. http://www.aacu.org/leap/hips

Kuhn, T. S. 1962. *The Structure of Scientific Revolutions*. Chicago: University of Chicago Press.

Kunda, Z. 1990. "The Case for Motivated Reasoning." *Psychological Bulletin* 108(3): 480–498.

Kyllonen, P. C. 2005. *The Case for Non-cognitive Assessments*. Princeton, NJ: ETS Research & Development, Educational Testing Service. https://www.ets.org/Media/Research/pdf/RD_Connections3.pdf

LeDoux, J. E. 1994. "Emotion, Memory and the Brain." *Scientific American*, June, 50–57.

LeDoux, J. E. 1996. *The Emotional Brain: The Mysterious Underpinnings of Emotional Life*. New York: Simon & Schuster.

LeDoux, J. E. 2002. *Synaptic Self: How Our Brains Become Who We Are*. New York: Penguin.

Lent, R. W., Brown, S. D., & Larkin, K. C. 1984. "Relation of Self-Efficacy Expectations to Academic Achievement and Persistence." *Journal of Counseling Psychology*, 31, 356–62.

Lent, R. W., Singley, D. Sheu, H., & Gainor, K. 2005. "Social Cognitive Predictors of Domain and Life Satisfaction: Exploring the Theoretical Precursors of Subjective Well-Being." *Journal of Counseling Psychology* 52(3): 429–442.

Levi, J., Segal, L., Laurant, R., Lang, A., & Rayburn, J. 2012. "F as in Fat: How Obesity Threatens America's Future." http://www.healthyamericans.org.

Levine, M. 2002. *A Mind at a Time*. New York: Simon & Schuster.

Levy, M. 2012. *Big Test for Corbett Loom in Election, Tax Credit*. New York: Associated Press.

Lickona, T. 1991. *Educating for Character: How Our Schools Can Teach Respect and Responsibility*. New York: Bantam Books.

Lickona, T., Schaps, E., & Lewis, C. 2003. "Eleven Principles of Effective Character Education." Accessed October 1, 2012. http://www.character.org/more-resources/ publications/11-principles.

Limber, S. P. 2004. "Implementation of the Olweus Bullying Prevention Program: Lessons Learned From the Field." In *Bullying in American Schools: A Social-Ecological Perspective on Prevention and Intervention*, edited by D. Espelage & S. Swearer, pp. 351–363. Mahwah, NJ: Lawrence Erlbaum.

Lobel, A. 1983. *Frog and Toad Together*. New York: HarperCollins.

Locke, B. "Need for Mental Health Awareness, Funding for College Students Grows." *Centre Daily Times*, May 21, 2016. http://www.centredaily.com/living/article79022677.html

Locker, J., & Cropley, M. 2004. "Anxiety, Depression and Self-Esteem in Secondary School Children: An Investigation Into the Impact of Standard Assessment Tests (SATs) and Other Important School Examinations." *School Psychology International* 25(3): 333–345.

Lopez, S. 2009. *Hope, Academic Success, and the Gallup Student Poll*. Omaha, NE: Gallup.

Lumina Foundation. 2015. *Who Is Today's Student?* https://www.luminafoundation.org/ todays-student-statistics

Magolda, M.B. (2010). "The Interweaving of Epistemological, Intrapersonal, and Interpersonal Development in the Evolution of Self-Authorship." In *Development and Assessment of Self-Authorship*, edited by M. B. Magolda, E. F. Creamer, & P. S. Meszaros, pp. 25–43. Sterling, VA: Stylus Publishing.

Mamun, A. 2003. *Life History of Cardiovascular Disease and Its Risk Factors—Multistate Life Table Approach and Application to the Framingham Heart Study*. Amsterdam: Rozenberg.

Mann, M., Hosman, C. M. H., Schaalma, H. P., & de Vries, N. K. 2004. "Self-Esteem in a Broad Spectrum Approach for Mental Health Promotion." *Health Education Research: Theory and Practice* 19(4): 357–372.

Marcia, J. E. 1966. "Development and Validation of the Ego Identity Status." *Journal of Personality and Social Psychology* 3: 551–558.

Marcia, J. E. 1991. "Identity and Self Development." In *Encyclopedia of Adolescence* (vol. 1), edited by R. Lerner, A. Peterson, & J. Brooks-Gunn. New York: Garland.

Marcia, J. E. 2002. "Identity and Psychosocial Development in Adulthood." *Identity: An International Journal of Theory and Research* 2: 7–28.142.

Marcia, J. E., Waterman, A. S., Matteson, D. R., Archer, S. L., & Orlofsky, J. L. 1993. *Ego Identity*. New York: Springer.

Marks, L. J., & Wade, J. C. 2015. "Positive Psychology on Campus: Creating the Conditions for Well-Being and Success," *About Campus*, January/February, pp. 9–15.

Markus, H. 1977. "Self-Schemata and Processing Information About the Self." *Journal of Personality and Social Psychology* 35: 63–78.

Markus, H., & Nurius, P. 1986. "Possible Selves." *American Psychologist* 41(9): 954–969.

Maslow, A. H. 1943. "A Theory of Human Motivation." *Psychological Review* 50: 370–396.

Maslow, A. H. 1954. *Motivation and Personality*. New York: Harper and Row.

Maslow, A. H. 1968. *Toward a Psychology of Being*. New York: John Wiley & Sons.

Masten, A. S., & Reed, M. J. 2005. "Resilience in Development." In *Handbook of Positive Psychology*, edited by C. R. Snyder & S. J. Lopez. New York: Oxford University Press.

Masters, J. C., Barden, R. C., & Ford, M. E. 1979. "Affective States, Expressive Behavior, and Learning in Children." *Journal of Personality and Social Psychology* 37: 380–390.

Mayo Clinic Staff. 2012. "Cognitive Behavioral Therapy." Accessed October 1, 2012. http://www.mayoclinic.com/health/cognitive-behavioral-therapy/MY00194.

McCarty, T. L., Wallace, S., Hadley Lynch, R., & Benally, A. 1991. "Classroom Inquiry and Navajo Learning Styles: A Call for Reassessment." *Anthropology and Education Quarterly* 22(1): 42–59.

McCombs, B. L. 2003. "A Framework for the Redesign of K–12 Education in the Context of Current Educational Reform." *Theory Into Practice* 42(2): 93–101.

McCullough, D. 2012. *You Are Not Special* (Video). Presented to graduating class, Wellesley High School, June 7. Accessed October 2, 2012. http://www.youtube.com/watch?v=_lfxYhtf8o4.

McDevitt, T. M., & Ormrod, J. E. 2007. *Child Development and Education*, 3rd ed. Upper Saddle River, NJ: Pearson Education.

McMeil, J. D. 2005. *Contemporary Curriculum: In Though and Action* (6th ed.). New York: John Wiley & Sons.

Miller, G. A. 2003. "The Cognitive Revolution: A Historical Perspective." *Trends in Cognitive Sciences* 7(3): 141–144.

Mink, O., Owen, K., & Mink, B. 1993. *Developing High-Performance People: The Art of Coaching*. Reading, MA: Addison-Wesley.

Moore, T. 1992. *Care of the Soul: A Guide For Cultivating Depth and Sacredness in Everyday Life*. New York: HarperCollins.

Moscovitch, M., & Craik, F. I. M. 1976. "Depth of Processing, Retrieval Cues, and Uniqueness of Encoding as a Factor in Recall." *Journal of Verbal Learning and Verbal Behavior* 15: 447–458.

Murphy, P. K., & Mason, L. 2006. "Changing Knowledge and Changing Beliefs." In *Handbook of Educational Psychology* (2nd ed.), edited by P. A. Alexander & P. Winne. New York: Lawrence Erlbaum.

National Alliance on Mental Illness. 2011. "Cognitive Behavioral Therapy Fact Sheet." Accessed October 1, 2012. http://www.nami.org/factsheets/CBT_factsheet.pdf.

National Association of Colleges and Employers. 2013. *The Professional Standards for College and University Career Services*. http://www.naceweb.org/knowledge/career-services-competencies.aspx

National Career Development Association (NACADA). 2005. *NACADA Statement of Core Values of Academic Advising*. http://www.nacada.ksu.edu/Resources/Clearinghouse/View-Articles/Core-values-of-academic-advising.aspx

National Career Development Association (NACADA). 2009. *National Career Development Guidelines (NCDG) Framework*. http://www.ncda.org/aws/NCDA/asset_manager/get_file/3384/ncdguidelines2007.pdf

National Center for Education Statistics. 2005a. "Dropout Rates in the United States: 2005." Accessed October 1, 2012. http://nces.ed.gov/pubs2007/dropout05/tables/table_A3.asp.

National Center for Education Statistics. 2005b. "National Assessment of Educational Progress—The Nation's Report Card." Accessed October 1, 2012. http://www.nces.ed.gov/nation'sreportcard.

National Center for Education Statistics. 2009. "Beginning Post-Secondary Students, Drop-Out Rates." Accessed October 1, 2012. http://nces.ed.gov/surveys/bps.

National Center for Education Statistics. 2011. "The Condition of Education 2011." Accessed October 1, 2012. http://nces.ed.gov/programs/coe/indicator_scr.asp.

National Commission on Excellence in Education (with D. Gardner). 1983. *A Nation at Risk: The Imperative for Educational Reform*. Washington, DC: U.S. Department of Education.

National Education Association. 2011. "Meeting the Needs of the Whole Child." Press release, April 29. Accessed October 2, 2012. http://help.senate.gov/newsroom/press/release/?id=aec51833-aa09–4f09-a354–2d5d493bae44&groups=Chair.

National Institute of Mental Health. 2010. "National Survey Confirms That Youth Are Disproportionately Affected by Mental Disorders." Accessed October 1, 2012. http://www.nimh.nih.gov/science-news/2010/national-survey-confirms-that-youth-are-disproportionately-affected-by-mental-disorders.shtml.

National Institute of Mental Health. 2011. "Borderline Personality Disorder Definition and Statistics." Accessed December 21, 2012. http://www.nimh.nih.gov/statistics/1Borderline.shtml.

National Survey of Student Engagement. 2007. *Experiences That Matter: Enhancing Student Learning and Success—Annual Results 2007*. Bloomington, IN: Indiana University Center for Postsecondary Research. http://nsse.indiana.edu/NSSE_2007_Annual_Report/docs/withhold/NSSE_2007_Annual_Report.pdf

National Survey of Student Engagement. 2013. *A Fresh Look at Student Engagement—Annual Results 2013*. Bloomington, IN: Indiana University Center for Postsecondary Research. http://nsse.indiana.edu/nsse_2013_results/pdf/nsse_2013_annual_results.pdf

National Survey of Student Engagement. 2015. *Engagement Insights: Survey Findings on the Quality of Undergraduate Education—Annual Results 2015*. Bloomington, IN: Indiana University Center for Postsecondary Research. http://nsse.indiana.edu/NSSE_2015_Results/pdf/NSSE_2015_Annual_Results.pdf

Neuman, S. B., Copple, C., & Bredekamp, S. 1998. "Learning to Read and Write: Developmentally Appropriate Practices for Young Children. A Joint Position Statement of the International Reading Association (IRA) and the National Association for the Education of Young Children (NAEYC), National Association for the Education of Young Children." Accessed October 2, 2012. http://oldweb.naeyc.org/about/positions/pdf/PSREAD98.PDF.

New Hampshire Department of Education. 2006. "New Hampshire Comprehensive Education Reform." Accessed October 2, 2012. http://www.ed.state.nh.us.education/EdReform/RWL.htm.

New Hampshire Department of Education. 2009. "Follow the Child Initiative." Accessed October 2, 2012. http://www.education.nh.gov/innovations/follow_child/documents/personal_ed.ppt.

Noddings, N. 2003. *Happiness and Education*. Cambridge: Cambridge University Press.

Noddings, N. 2005. *Educating Citizens for Global Awareness*. New York: Teachers College Press.

Noddings, N. 2006. *Critical Lessons: What Our Schools Should Teach*. New York: Cambridge University Press.

Northeast Foundation for Children. 2012. "Responsive Classroom." Accessed October 2, 2012. http://www.responsiveclassroom.org/about-responsive-classroom.

Northwest Evaluation Association. 2005. *RIT Scale Norms for Use With Achievement Level Tests and Measures of Academic Progress.* Lake Oswego, OR: Northwest Evaluation Association.

Odum, H. T. 1988. "Self-Organization, Transformity, and Information." *Science* 242: 1132–1139.

Ogden, C. L., Carroll, M. D., Kit, B. K., & Flegal, K. M. 2012. "Prevalence of Obesity and Trends in Body Mass Index Among U.S. Children and Adolescents, 1999–2010." *Journal of the American Medical Association* 307(5): 483–490.

Ohio State University. 2015. *Office of Student Life Wellness Assessment.* http://cssl.osu.edu/posts/documents/wellness-assessment-report-january-2015.pdf

Ormrod, J. E. 2011. *Essentials of Educational Psychology* (3rd ed.). Upper Saddle River, NJ: Pearson Education.

Orth, U., Robbins, R. W., & Widaman, K. F. 2012. "Life-Span Development of Self-Esteem and Its Effects on Important Life Outcomes." *Journal of Personality and Social Psychology* 102(6): 1271–1288.

Oyserman, D., & James, L. 2009. "Possible Selves: From Content to Process." In *The Handbook of Imagination and Mental Stimulation*, edited by K. D. Markman, W. M. Klein, & J. A. Suhr. New York: Psychology Press.

Parjares, M. F. 1992. "Teachers Beliefs and Educational Research: Cleaning Up a Messy Construct." *Review of Educational Research* 62: 307–332.

Parjares, M. F. 1996. "Self-Efficacy Beliefs in Academic Settings." *Review of Educational Research* 66(4): 543–578.

Pastor, P. N., Reuben, C. A., & Duran, C. R. 2012. "Identifying Emotional and Behavioral Problems in Children Aged 4–17 Years: United States, 2001–2007." *National Health Statistic Report*, February 24. Atlanta, GA: Centers for Disease Control and Prevention, Office of Analysis and Epidemiology. http://www.cdc.gov/nchs/data/nhsr/nhsr048.pdf.

Patrick, H., Ryan, A. M., & Kaplan, A. 2007. "Early Adolescent Perceptions of the Classroom Social Environment, Motivational Beliefs, and Engagement." *Journal of Educational Psychology* 99(1): 83–98.

Pekrun, R. 1992. "The Impact of Emotions on Learning and Achievement: Towards a Theory of Cognitive/Motivational Mediators." *Applied Psychology: An International Review* 41(4): 359–376.

Pekrun, R. 2000. "A Social-Cognitive, Control-Value Theory of Achievement Emotions." *Advances in Psychology* 131: 143–163.

Pekrun, R., Goetz, T., Titz, W., & Perry, R. P. 2002. "Academic Emotions in Students' Self-Regulated Learning and Achievement: A Program of Qualitative and Quantitative Research." *Educational Psychologist* 37(2): 91–105.

Pennsylvania Department of Education. 2005. "Pennsylvania Department of Education Press Release." http://www.pdenewsroom.state.pa.us.

Peterson, L. E., Stahlberg, D., & Dauenheimer, D. 2000. "Effects of Self-Schema Elaboration on Affective and Cognitive Reactions to Self-Relevant Information." *Genetic, Social, and General Psychology Monographs* 26: 25–42.

Piaget, J. 1936. *Origins of Intelligence in the Child.* London: Routledge & Kegan Paul.

Piaget, J. 1957. *Construction of Reality in the Child.* London: Routledge & Kegan Paul.

Piaget, J. 1968. *Six Psychological Studies.* New York: Random House.

Pintrich, P. R. 1999. "The Role of Motivation in Promoting and Sustaining Self-Regulated Learning." *International Journal of Educational Research* 31: 459–470.

Pintrich, P. R., & de Groot, E. 1990. "Motivational and Self-Regulated Learning Components of Classroom Academic Performance." *Journal of Educational Psychology* 82(1): 33–50.

Pintrich, P. R., & Schunk, D. H. 2002. *Motivation in Education: Theory, Research, and Applications.* Upper Saddle River, NJ: Prentice-Hall.

Pintrich, P. R., Marx, R. W., & Boyle, R. A. 1993. "Beyond Cold Conceptual Change: The Role of Motivational Beliefs and Classroom Contextual Factors in the Process of Conceptual Change." *Review of Educational Research* 63: 167–199.

Plato. 1993. *Phaedo.* New York: Oxford University Press.

Psychology Campus. 2011. "Existential Therapy Definition." Accessed October 2, 2012. http://www.psychologycampus.com/psychology-counseling/existential-therapy.html.

Public Broadcasting Service. 2012. "Finding Your Roots: Samuel L. Jackson, Condoleezza Rice, & Ruth Simmons." Accessed October 2, 2012. http://video.pbs.org/video/2225130612.

Putnam, R. 1993. *Making Democracy Work: Civic Tradition in Modern Italy.* Princeton, NJ: Princeton University Press.

Reeder, G. D., McCormick, C. B., & Esselman, E. D. 1987. "Self-Referent Processing and Recall of Prose." *Journal of Educational Psychology* 79(3): 243–248.

Republican Party of Texas. 2012. "Report of Platform Committee and Rules Committee." Accessed October 2, 2012. http://www.tfn.org/site/DocServer/2012-Platform-Final.pdf?docID=3201.

Resnick, L. B., & Resnick, D. P. 1992. "Assessing the Thinking Curriculum: New Tools for Educational Reform." In *Changing Assessments: Alternative Views of Aptitude, Achievement, and Instruction,* edited by B. R. Gifford & M. C. O'Connor, pp. 37–75. Boston: Kluwer.

Reyna, V. 2002. "What Is Scientifically Based Evidence? What Is Its Logic?" Paper presented at U.S. Department of Education Scientifically Based Research Conference. Accessed October 2, 2012. http://www.ed.gov/nclb/methods/whatworks/research/index.html.

Robinson, K. 2001. *Out of Our Minds: Learning to Be Creative.* West Sussex: Capstone.

Rogers, C. 1954. "Toward a Theory of Creativity." *ETC: A Review of General Semantics* 11: 249–260.

Rogers, C. 1961. *On Becoming a Person.* Boston: Houghton Mifflin.

Rogers, C. 1980. *A Way of Being.* Boston: Houghton Mifflin.

Rogers, C. 1986. "A Client-Centered/Person-Centered Approach to Therapy." In *The Carl Rogers Reader,* edited by H. Kirschenbaum & V. Land Henderson. Boston: Houghton Mifflin.

Rogers, P. 2011. *Understanding Risk and Protective Factors for Suicide: A Primer for Preventing Suicide.* Washington, DC: Substance Abuse and Mental Health Services Administration (SAMSHA) Suicide Prevention Resource Center (SPRC). http://www.sprc.org/sites/sprc.org/files/library/RiskProtectiveFactorsPrimer.pdf

Rogers, T. B. 1981. "A Model of the Self as an Aspect of the Human Information Processing System." In *Personality, Cognition, and Social Interaction,* edited by N. Cantor & J. F. Kihlstrom, pp. 193–214. Hillsdale, NJ: Lawrence Erlbaum.

Rogers, T. B., Kuiper, N. A., & Kirker, W. S. 1977. "Self-Reference and the Encoding of Personal Information." *Journal of Personality and Social Psychology* 35: 677–688.

Rosenbaum, P. R. 2002. *Observational Studies* (2nd ed.). New York: Springer.

Rotter, J. B. 1966. "Generalized Expectancies for Internal Versus External Control of Reinforcement." *Psychological Monographs* 80(1): 1–28.

Ryan, R. M., & Deci, E. 2000. "Self-Determination Theory and the Facilitation of Intrinsic Motivation, Social Development, and Well-Being." *American Psychologist* 55: 68–78.

Ryan, R. M., & Deci, E. L. 2001. "On Happiness and Human Potentials: A Review of Research on Hedonic and Eudaimonic Well-Being." *Annual Review of Psychology* 52: 141–166.

Ryff, C. D., & Singer, B. 1998a. "The Contours of Positive Human Health." *Psychological Inquiry* 9: 1–28.

Ryff, C. D., & Singer, B. 1998b. "The Role of Purpose in Life and Personal Growth in Positive Human Health." In *The Human Quest for Meaning: A Handbook of Psychological Research and Clinical Applications*, edited by P. T. P. Wong & P. S. Fry, pp. 213–235. Mahwah, NJ: Lawrence Erlbaum.

Ryff, C. D., & Singer, B. 2003. "The Role of Emotion on Pathways to Positive Health." In *Handbook of Affective Sciences*, edited by R. J. Davidson, K. R. Scherer, & H. H. Goldsmith. New York: Oxford University Press.

Ryff, C. D., Singer, B., Love, G. D., & Essex, M. J. 1998. "Resilience in Adulthood and Later Life: Defining Features and Dynamic Processes." In *Handbook of Aging and Mental Health*, edited by J. Lomranz. New York: Plenum.

Scheffler, I. 1985. *Of Human Potential*. Boston: Routledge & Kegan Paul.

Schreiner L., & Anderson, E. 2005. Strengths based advising: A new lens for higher education. *NACADA Journal*, 25(2), 20–29.

Schroeder, S. 2007. "We Can Do Better: Improving the Health of the American People." *New England Journal of Medicine* 357: 1221–1228.

Schunk, D. H. 2000. *Learning Theories: An Educational Perspective* (3rd ed.). Columbus, OH: Merrill/Prentice-Hall.

Seifert, T. A. 2005. *The Ryff Scales of Psychological Well-Being*. Center for Inquiry at Wabash University. http://www.liberalarts.wabash.edu/ryff-scales/

Seligman, M. E. P. 2011. *Flourish: A Visionary New Understanding of Happiness and Well-Being*. New York: Free Press.

Seligman, M. E. P., & Csikszentmihalyi, M. 2000. "Positive Psychology: An Introduction." *American Psychologist* 55: 5–14.

Seligman, M. E. P., Schulman, P., DeRubeis, R. J., & Hollon, S. D. (1999). "The Prevention of Depression and Anxiety." *Prevention & Treatment*, 2(1), December: 8a. http://dx.doi.org/10.1037/1522-3736.2.1.28a

Selingo, J. 2015. *Student Success: Building a Culture for Retention and Completion on College Campuses*. Washington, DC: The Chronicle of Higher Education.

Senge, P., Cambron-McCabe, N., Lucas, T., Smith, B., Dutton, J., & Kleiner, A. 2000. *Schools That Learn*. New York: Doubleday.

Shanahan, M. J. 2000. "Pathways to Adulthood in Changing Societies: Variability and Mechanisms in Life Course Perspective." *Annual Review of Sociology* 26: 667–692.

Shankman, M. L., Allen, S. J., and Miguel, R. 2015. *Emotionally Intelligent Leadership for Students: Inventory*, 2nd ed. San-Francisco: Jossey-Bass

Shaw, G. B. 1962. *Man and Superman*. New York: Heritage Press.

Shouse, E. 2005 "Feeling, Emotion, Affect." Accessed October 2, 2012. http://journal.media-culture.org.au/0512/03-shouse.php.

Sigel, I. E. 1985. "Parental Concepts of Development." In *Parental Belief Systems: The Psychological Consequences for Children*, edited by I. E. Sigel, pp. 83–105. Hillsdale, NJ: Lawrence Erlbaum.

Silko, L. M. 1996. *Yellow Woman and a Beauty of the Spirit Essays*. New York: Simon & Schuster.

Silvergate, H. (2016). "Harvard to Supply Life's Meaning to Students." *Minding the Campus*, March. http://www.mindingthecampus.org/2016/03/harvard-to-supply-lifes-meaning-to-students/

Smith, E. R., Simpson, J. A., & King, L. A. 2012. "Life-Span Development of Self-Esteem and Its Effects on Important Life Outcomes." *Journal of Personality and Social Psychology* 77: 1271–1288.

Snyder, C. R., & Lopez, S. J. 2002. *Handbook of Positive Psychology*. London: Oxford University Press.

Snyder, C. R., & Lopez, S. J., eds. 2005. *Handbook of Positive Psychology.* London: Oxford University Press.

Snyder, C. R., Rand, K. L., & Sigmon, D. R. 2005. "Hope Theory: A Member of the Positive Psychology Family." In *Handbook of Positive Psychology*, edited by C. R. Snyder & S. J. Lopez, pp. 257–276. London: Oxford University Press.

Sparks, S. D. 2012. "Neuroscientists Find Learning Is Not 'Hard-Wired.'" *Education Week*, June 6.

Speer, L. 2012. "2012 Kids Count Data Book." Accessed October 2, 2012. http://datacenter.kidscount.org/DataBook/2012/OnlineBooks/KIDSCOUNT2012DataBookFullReport.pdf.

Spiegel, D., Loewenstein, R. J., Lewis-Fernandez, R., Vedat, S., Simeon, D., Vermetten, E., Etzel Carden, E., & Dell, P. F. 2011. "Dissociative Disorders in DSM-5." *Depression and Anxiety* 28: 824–852.

St. Petersburg College. 2015. *The College Experience*. http://www.spcollege.edu/collegeexperience/

St. Petersburg College. 2016. *My Learning Plan.* Student success white paper. http://www.spcollege.edu/SACS_COC/artifacts/2.10_Student_Support_Services/MyLearningPlanWhitepaper.pdf

Stanford University. 2016. *Designing Your Life*. http://www.stanford.edu/class/me104b/cgi-bin/

Sternberg, L. 2007. "Who Are the Bright Children? The Cultural Context of Being and Acting Intelligent." *Educational Researcher* 36(3): 148–155.

Sternberg, R. J. 1999. *Handbook of Creativity*. New York: Cambridge University Press.

Sternberg, R. J. 2013. "Research to Improve Retention Inside Higher Ed." https://www.insidehighered.com/views/2013/02/07/essay-use-research-improve-student-retention#ixzz2QAelwRP5

Sternberg, R. J., & Lubart, T. I. 1995. *Defying the Crowd: Cultivating Creativity in a Culture of Conformity*. New York: Free Press.

Strauss, A., & Corbin, J. 1998. *Basics of Qualitative Research: Techniques and Procedures for Developing Grounded Theory*. Thousand Oaks, CA: Sage.

Strauss, R. S. 2000. "Childhood Obesity and Self-Esteem." *Pediatrics* 105(1): e15. Accessed October 2, 2012. http://www.pediatrics.org/cgi/content/full/105/1/e15.

Substance Abuse and Mental Health Services Administration. 2011. "Results From the 2010 National Survey on Drug Use and Health: Summary of National Findings." NSDUH Series H-41, HHS Publication no. (SMA) 11–4658. Rockville, MD: Substance Abuse and Mental Health Services Administration.

Suicide Prevention Resource Center. 2014. *Suicide among College and University Students in the United States*. Waltham, MA: Education Development Center.

Swarbrick, M. 2006. "A Wellness Approach." *Psychiatric Rehabilitation Journal* 29(4): 311–14.

Taylor Huber, M., & Hutchings, P. 2004. *Integrative Learning: Mapping the Terrain*. Washington, DC: Association of American Colleges and Universities and the Carnegie Foundation for the Advancement of Teaching. http://archive.carnegiefoundation.org/pdfs/elibrary/elibrary_pdf_636.pdf

Ternouth, A., Collier, D., & Maughan, B. 2009. "Childhood Emotional Problems and Self-Perceptions Predict Weight Gain in a Longitudinal Regression Model." *BMC Medicine* 7: 46.

The Pennsylvania State University. 2014. *PSU High Impact Practice: Greening of Philadelphia* Service Learning. http://h2oblues.org/themes/penn-state/penn-state-philadelphia-event

The Pennsylvania State University. 2016. *The Pennsylvania State University's Strategic Plan for 2016 to 2020*. http://www.psu.edu/trustees/pdf/Penn%20State%20Strategic%20Plan%202016-2020%20-%20CoGLRP%20Review%2001-04-16.pdf

Tinto, V. 2004. "Linking Learning and Leaving." In *Reworking the Student Departure Puzzle*, edited by J. M. Braxton. Nashville, TN: Vanderbilt University Press.

Toffler, A. 1970. *Future Shock*. New York: Bantam Books.

Toffler, A. 1980. *The Third Wave: The Classic Study of Tomorrow*. New York: Bantam Books.

Tomasello, M. 2000. *The Cultural Origins of Human Cognition*. Cambridge, MA: Harvard University Press.

Twenge, J. M., & Campbell, K. W. 2009. *The Narcissism Epidemic: Living in the Age of Entitlement*. New York: Free Press.

Twenge, J. M., Gentile, B., DeWall, C. N., Ma, D. S., Lacefield, K., & Schurtz, D. R. 2010. "Birth Cohort Increases in Psychopathology Among Young Americans, 1938–2007: A Cross-Temporal Meta-Analysis of the MMPI." *Clinical Psychology Review* 30: 145–154.

Tyack, D., & Cuban, L. 1995. *Tinkering Toward Utopia*. Cambridge, MA: Harvard University Press.

U.S. Congress. *Public Law 89–10/Elementary and Secondary Education Act of 1965*, 89th Cong., 1st sess. v. 79. Washington, DC: GPO.

U.S. Department of Education. 2002. "No Child Left Behind Fact Sheet." Accessed October 2, 2012. http://www.ed.gov/offices/OESE/esea/factsheet.html.

U.S. Department of Education. 2009. "Evaluation of Evidence-Based Practices in Online Learning: A Meta-Analysis and Review of Online Learning Studies." Accessed October 2, 2012. http://www2.ed.gov/rschstat/eval/tech/evidence-based-practices/finalreport.pdf.

U.S. Department of Education. 2010. "Learning Powered by Technology." Accessed October 2, 2012. http://www.ed.gov/technology/netp-2010.

U.S. Department of Health and Human Services. 2012. "Healthy People 2020." Accessed October 1, 2012. http://www.healthypeople.gov/2020/connect/webinars.aspx.

U.S. Department of Education, National Center for Education Statistics. 2011. "The Condition of Education 2011." Accessed October 2, 2012. http://nces.ed.gov/programs/coe/indicator_scr.asp.

U.S. Department of Education, Office of Elementary and Secondary Education. 2001. *No Child Left Behind: A Desktop Reference*. Washington, DC: U.S. Department of Education.

University of Central Florida. 2016. "Counseling and Psychological Services: Therapist Assisted Online (TAO)." http://caps.sdes.ucf.edu/tao

University of Michigan. 2010. "Monitoring the Future, A Response to the Epidemic of Prescription Drug Use." Accessed October 2, 2012. http://www.whitehouse.gov/sites/default/files/ondcp/Fact_Sheets/prescription_drug_abuse_fact_sheet_4–25–11.pdf.

University of Michigan. 2016a. "Newnan Academic Advising Center Student Success Workshops." http://www.lsa.umich.edu/advising/academicsupport/strategiesforsuccess/healthandwellness

University of Michigan. 2016b. "Integrative Learning in Student Life." https://studentlife.umich.edu/research/article/integrative-learning-student-life-part-iii

University of Michigan. 2016c. "Integrative Learning in Student Life: Student Life Research Video." https://studentlife.umich.edu/integrative-learning

Urdan, T., & Schoenfelder, E. 2006. "Classroom Effects on Student Motivation: Goal Structures, Social Relationships, and Competence Beliefs." *Journal of School Psychology* 44: 331–349.

Van Geert, P., & Steenbeek, H. 2008. "Brains and the Dynamics of Wants and Cans in Learning." *Mind, Brain, and Education* 2(2): 62–66.

Varney, J. (2012). "Proactive (Intrusive) Advising!" *Academic Advising Today*, 35(3; September). http://www.nacada.ksu.edu/Resources/Academic-Advising-Today/View-Articles/Proactive-(Intrusive)-Advising!.aspx#

Vygotsky, L. S. 1978. *Mind in Society*. Cambridge, MA: Harvard University Press.

Vygotsky, L. S. 1987. "Thinking and Speech." In *The Collective Works of L. S. Vygotsky*, translated by N. Minick and edited by R. W. Weber & A. S. Caron. New York: Plenum Press.

Wade, J. C., Marks, L. I., & Hetzel, R. D. (eds.). 2015. *Positive Psychology on the College Campus*. New York: Oxford University Press.

Wallace, J. 2011. "Supt. Marple Lays Out Wide-Ranging Plans for Lawmakers." *The Legislature*, June 30. Accessed October 2, 2012. http://publications.wvsba.org/2011/06/30/news.

Wallis, C. 2005. "The New Science of Happiness." *Time*, January 17. http://content.time.com/time/magazine/article/0,9171,1015832,00.html

Wechsler, H., McKenna, M. L., Less, S. M., & Dietz, W. H. 2004. "The Role of Schools in Preventing Childhood Obesity." Accessed October 2, 2012. http://www.cdc.gov/healthyyouth/physicalactivity/pdf/roleofschools_obesity.pdf.

Weinert, F. E. 1987. "Introduction and Overview: Metacognition and Motivation as Determinants of Effective Learning and Understanding." In *Metacognition, Motivation, and Understanding*, edited by F. E. Weinert & R. H. Kluwe. Hillsdale, NJ: Lawrence Erlbaum.

Wells, G. 1986. *The Meaning Makers: Children Learning Language and Using Language to Learn*. Portsmouth, NH: Heinemann.

West Virginia State Legislature. 2011. *Senate Bill Number 516* (Requiring state board establish digital learning program). Accessed October 2, 2012. http://www.legis.state.wv.us/bill_status/Bills_history.cfm?input=516&year=2011&sessiontype=RS&btype=bill.

Wigfield, A., Eccles, J. S., Yoon, K. S., Harold, R. D., Arberton, A. J. A., Feedman-Doan, C., & Blumenfeld, P. 1997. "Change in Children's Competence Beliefs and Subjective Task Values Across the Elementary School Years: A 3-Year Study." *Journal of Educational Psychology* 89(3): 451–469.

Wilkins, J. 2015. *Students' Perceptions of their First-Year Experience in Relation to Support They Receive from an Urban Mid-sized Public College*. Internal study and presentation. joshuawilkin@gmail.com

Willoughby, C. 2015. "Theoretical Design and Real World Outcomes for New Student Orientation." Presented at the Theory to Practice to Outcomes: Connecting Student Development Theory to Community College Practice Conference, Morgan State University, Maryland.

Willoughby, C. 2016a. *Student Success at Butler County Community College*. Internal white paper.

Willoughby, C. 2016b. *BC3 Welcome Day 2013–2014 Report*. Internal white paper.

Winston, R. B., Jr., Miller, T. K., Ender, S. C., Grites, T. J., & associates (eds.). 1984. *Developmental Academic Advising*. San Francisco: Jossey-Bass.

Wolf, A. M., & Colditz, G. A. 1994. "The Cost of Obesity: The U.S. Perspective." *Pharmacoeconomics* 5(Suppl. 1): 34–37.

Wolf, A. M., & Colditz, G. A. 1998. "Current Estimates of the Economic Cost of Obesity in the United States." *Obesity Research* 6(2): 97–106.

Woolfolk, A. 2004. *Educational Psychology* (9th ed.). Boston: Pearson Education.

Yancy, K. B. 2004. *Teaching Literature as Reflective Practice*. Urbana, IL: National Council of Teachers of English.

Yazzie-Mintz, E. 2010. "Schools Are Responding to Latest Findings From the High School Survey of Student Engagement." Indiana University, School of Education Feature Topic. Accessed October 2, 2012. http://education/indiana.edu/Feature_Topic_Detail/tabid/11553/Default.aspx?xmid=3554.

Zentner, M., & Renaud, O. 2007. "Origins of Adolescents Ideal Self: An Intergenerational Perspective." *Journal of Personality and Social Psychology* 92(3): 357–375.

About the Authors

Henry G. Brzycki, Ph.D., has more than 30 years of experience providing leadership to the fields of education and psychology. Dr. Brzycki challenges scholars and practitioners to expand their boundaries of understanding in order to impact the quality of people's lives. Dr. Brzycki is considered the leading authority on how to produce student mental health and well-being outcomes through schooling.

Dr. Brzycki founded The Brzycki Group, where his innovative counseling and psychoeducational programs pioneered positive psychology and strengths-based counseling methods. Dr. Brzycki consults to schools, colleges, foundations, and policy makers on how to realize the potential of people. Most recently he founded The Center for the Self in Schools. The Center's non-profit mission is to impact the psychological, socioemotional, and physical well-being of K–16 students through outreach programs, professional development, and self-knowledge curricula.

Dr. Brzycki earned his M.A. from Tufts University and his Ph.D. from The Pennsylvania State University. He is co-author with Elaine Brzycki of the best-selling book *Student Success in Higher Education: Developing the Whole Person through High-Impact Practices*. He is also author of a best-selling academic book, *The Self in Schooling: Theory and Practice—How to Create Happy, Healthy, Flourishing Children in the 21st Century*, which captures his insights and experiences as a counselor, teacher, and thought leader, and offers a breakthrough model for transforming people's lives, counseling and teaching and learning best practices, and our society.

Elaine J. Brzycki, Ed.M., coauthored *Student Success in Higher Education: Developing the Whole Person through High-Impact Practices*, which offers a breakthrough model for transforming people's lives through educational best practices. Cofounder of The Brzycki Group & The Center for the Self in Schools, Brzycki currently serves on the Board to lead outreach and strategically guide the future of educational services. Brzycki graduated from Wellesley College as a Wellesley Scholar and attended Oxford University in England. She co-developed many of The Brzycki Group's leading programs while earning her Ed.M. at the Harvard University Graduate School of Education.

Brzycki has more than 25 years of experience as an educator and a higher education administrator. She is committed to empowering young people's self-expression and greatness, and to sharing wisdom between generations.

About The Brzycki Group & The Center for the Self in Schools

Mission and Work in the World for More Than 30 Years

We have been on a lifelong journey of self-discovery, together. The deeper our respective inquiries into our inner selves, the closer we feel to each other, and connected to our true selves. We have been hungry for living life fully, with the ability to experience our experiences—in other words, "sucking the marrow out of life!" This is how we came upon the wisdom of humankind to inform our quest, to satisfy our own needs for happiness, wellness, and meaning.

The "self" may be defined as the essential or particular qualities that distinguish one person from another, such as personality traits or talents. However, it can be even more useful in teaching, learning, and counseling to think of the self as a holistic system with three major components: the body, the mind, and the soul. Further, learning about the self is really the same in both traditional classroom educational settings and therapeutic counseling, in that the pathway to learning is through psychological processes that are personally meaningful. In both environments, the goal is similar: to lay the groundwork for a flourishing life. The root of the word psychology, "psyc," comes from the Greek word "psyche," which means soul. In the context of psychology, the mind is "an organic system reaching all parts of the body and serving to adjust the total organism to the demands of the environment" (Friend & Guralnik, 1953, p. 1175). All these aspects of the person unite as the self. The self is important to know and understand because it mediates the inner life with the outer life to determine our realities and shape a positive life course.

During our own journey to discover greater meaning, life purpose, and mental and physical well-being in our lives, and through our commitment to give back to others, we have studied the self in K–16 classroom learning and therapeutic counseling contexts. We realized every one of our breakthroughs in our own understanding of our lives occurred because we had access to a new level of self-understanding and higher consciousness. The quality of our lives soared every time we examined our life and learned more about ourselves.

At one transformative moment that came to Henry well into his adult years, when he felt at one with the goodness of humanity, it occurred to him that others might find this process of self-discovery as valuable and enlightening as we had. We then began to think about our own education through the public school system and which lessons helped us to live a high-quality life and manifest our unique potential during and after our schooling. In particular, we examined which lessons we learned—or had not learned—about ourselves.

Certainly, we learned much about the usual academic content—and we enjoyed most—although we did not understand why we were learning much of it. While Henry was reading, for example, *The Catcher in the Rye* or *Walden* in English literature class in high school, he did not know how to make these brilliant works, with their deep and meaningful thoughts and concepts, relevant to his life, to his own self-understanding. As a developing adolescent, he hungered for this type of meaning. He was not getting what he needed from his teachers to appreciate the depth of the academic content, nor was he learning how to apply these meanings to his own personal development and life-course trajectory. Then, during senior year, Henry's physics teacher started off the first semester by asserting that we did not need him, that all that his students needed to learn was already in ourselves and our textbook. Well, after 12 years of schooling during which Henry was taught to be reliant if not dependent on teachers for his future success, this myth and belief system was shattered, thankfully.

Henry remembers the first time he experienced a transformation in his own understanding of his unique journey toward self-actualization: he was sitting in a freshman organizational psychology class. Simply upon seeing Maslow's Hierarchy of Needs (1954), he felt as though his head exploded. He learned that powerful personal development can occur through the teaching of academic content.

On the basis of these discoveries, we were compelled to design a series of educational courses that transformed the lives of our students and counseling clients through self-understanding. With numerous years of successfully transforming the lives of clients, healing their psychological conditions, and using this model of personal transformation to flourish personally and professionally, we realized that our educational system could be better utilized to empower young people to live a high quality of life, filled with personal meaning, positive life directions, and psychological and physical well-being. If we included these goals in our education system, then, just maybe, we could make the world a better place.

Who among us has gone through life without knowing who we are, or without having a paradigm to guide us in understanding who we are and why we do the things we do? Perhaps if we had known who we were, we could have accessed deeper experiences in our relationships. We could have had more accomplishments academically and better job prospects that more closely mirrored our innate nature and talents. By gaining a more thorough understanding of our unique potential, we can find a more direct pathway to reaching it as we navigate this fast-paced modern life, characterized by rapid change. During the times in which overwhelming personal and professional crises threaten our mental and physical health, we must find the psychological and emotional tools we need to get through these periods.

We have dedicated our lives to studying and empowering the self from numerous perspectives. In our K–16 teaching counseling practice, we have worked with clients seeking guidance to choose a college, change careers, conquer substance abuse, overcome marriage and family dysfunction, and recover from sexual abuse, among others. The one common denominator that we have found in all cases is that the pathway to success—whether it be academic and career success, emotional and psychological healing, or inner peace and love—is through a better understanding of one's self and making one's self-awareness a high priority.

As counselors and teachers, we must be interested in studying how to make a difference in the lives of the young people in our care and how to empower them through our work. This is where these two human service professions come together at the mission level—to educate and to help individuals become themselves. We share a mission to empower the life course in terms of health and well-being, and these are learned and manifest through personally meaningful experiences.

We want to connect and deepen the processes that these two professions use in their respective strategies for reaching people: counselors' interventions and teachers' lesson activities. The common factor to producing successful results in both domains—whether a student is learning academic content in a classroom or a client is experiencing a productive session on how to be happy and experience authentic emotions in a therapist's office—is self-understanding. Over the years, we became aware that our professional effectiveness in both professional arenas was based on our ability to help both our students and clients learn about themselves.

The research is compelling and persuasive about the causal links between the psychology of the self, psychological and physical well-being, and academic achievement. Numerous studies from the psychological and medical professions demonstrate the direct causal relationship between self-esteem and depression and obesity, purpose in life and emotional well-being, and self-efficacy and positive life-course trajectories, among other examples presented throughout this *Toolkit* (Bandura et al., 2001; CDC, 2012; Cohen, 2006; Goetz et al., 2003; Locker & Cropley, 2004; Mann et al.,

2004; Orth et al., 2012; Ryan & Deci, 2000; Ryff & Singer, 1998a; 1998b; Ternouth et al., 2009). The Adverse Childhood Experiences (ACE) study provides an inter-disciplinary view when researching the causal relationship between adverse child-hood experiences, social-emotional and cognitive impairment, adverse or health risk behaviors, disease, disability and social problems, and life expectancy (Felitti et al., 1998; Felitti & Anda, 2009).

As we teach numerous distinctions about the self in our classrooms, children should emerge from their schooling experiences more able to be well, with a greater under-standing of what it means to be healthy—emotionally, physically, spiritually, intel-lectually, and psychologically. Academic learning and success will stem from student well-being and contribute to it, rather than being the sole purpose of schooling or occurring without regard to larger mental health concerns.

As counselors, teachers, and education leaders, we have applied the ideas presented here in this *Toolkit*, with transformational results in terms of the quality of people's lives and their psychological and physical well-being. We believe that the idea of teaching self-knowledge to all through education to improve mental and physical well-being represents a breakthrough in what it means to be human, with all the inherent possibilities for a better life, for everyone. In short, focusing on the self in education is an idea whose time has come.

What is transformative about our work and the three high-impact mental health and well-being practices is that we demonstrate through research and practice that students have a higher purpose that is driving their thoughts, feelings, and actions, a DNA of consciousness that, when learned, transforms their quality of life.

Professional Development from The Brzycki Group & The Center for the Self in Schools

At the time of publication, the following resources are available. For the most up-to-date information about these resources, please visit www.BrzyckiGroup.com.

- Professional development workshops on the Integrated Self Model (iSelf), Self Across the Curriculum, the Success Predictor, the Champions Program, and the Vision Course for Adolescents—Participate through face-to-face delivery at your school, or via online meeting platforms
- Presentations to your school staff at in-service sessions; school board; commu-nity at large

- Web-based workshops and seminars—One-on-one coaching to learn methods to help students create good well-being choices and design success pathways. Receive handouts, planning sheets, and examples of student-centered lessons. Confidential student case and student-parent sessions to address particular issues.
- Bulk orders—Order 10 or more copies of the *Toolkit* or our other books and qualify for a 20% discount.
- Social media—Follow updates at our website and on Twitter @iSelfmodel.

We always enjoy receiving feedback from teachers, counselors, parents and students on your successes; please let us share in your positive lives and the difference you are making. We would also enjoy hearing about your Success Predictor hierarchies to see how you are constructing the distinctions and views of success. Share your thoughts via email correspondence: henry@brzyckigroup.com and elaine@brzyckigroup.com.

www.ingramcontent.com/pod-product-compliance
Lightning Source LLC
Chambersburg PA
CBHW081419270326
41931CB00015B/3328